New Hiking Trail Cast Shadow on the Tattooed

New Hiking Trail Cast Shadow on the Tattooed

E Lloyd Kelly

CONTENTS

1

New Hiking Trail Cast Shadow on the Tattooed
A Novel: Real Inky Trails book series

Introduction

"Raw, Real, and Full of Fun." New Hiking Trail Cast Shadow on the Tattooed is a work of fiction. Born out of some fool's wild imagination, told in wry humor, and a feeble attempt at poetry. Yes, wordplay is the order of the day around here, too. Snippets of Jamaican Patois were inserted here and there throughout, as may be found fitting. Yeah, man, a Jamaica yaad mi cum fram, sorry, I meant to say, I'm Jamaican born and bred—okay?

These well-sculptured, firm-bodied Cekko-warrior girls traverse diverse dimensions astride long-legged Zebra-striped beasts searching for the lost Genodes. Dishing out their brand of peace and passivity liberally along the way, not even special agent Shadow was to be spared. Yes, Shadow casting was a regular, everyday occurrence in the Cekkoland sphere. He was force-pushed out into the humanoid spheres, and now, look. Look at what they have gone and done...

Chapter 1: Trouble Is Brewing.

Imagine with me, will you?

Imagine that just like the Cekko people, you've got the special powers, and the ability to go on for long periods without sleeping, even for an hour, eating, or doing anything else as normal people do. Imagine that with all of that, you can still function at your peak and stay focused and alert. And there you are at a vantage point where you are hanging out suspended somewhere outside the conference room properly. Just out of sight, and out of their knowledge of you being there. But you're (nonetheless) there, eavesdropping on the meeting and spying in on the conversation. Trying to see what's going on and hear what you can hear. You're there listening in on it. Look, look at the king, he's sitting on the throne, there, in his royal chair. He's a bit slumped in his posture today, not his usual majestic self. He's distressed, even biting his nails. Or more like pretending not to be, biting. He's (obviously) more than a bit troubled. Everybody who is anybody in the hierarchy of the kingdom is there. They're all there and sitting in their respective places in a semicircle at the conference table, facing the king. Everybody, including the chief ranger, Smokey, is there. Some of his most promising prospects of the year are there, too. Shadow is there for sure, and the young trainee whose name is Beahon. The girls, "ONE." Onella, Noella, and Estella are there. It would be interesting to hear what they are talking about. What's on the menu for discussion today, waiting to be dished out? Now your curiosity is getting the better of you, so you're inching in closer. There's a crack in the windowpane; you've noticed it for sure. You're now edging your way there nimbly along the ledge just outside the window on the same floor as the conference room. Because of the prevailing conditions, yes, it's dark outside, and because you're wearing dark clothing yourself. You're confident that you will remain concealed from their view and get to make it all the way there. Still standing upright on those shaky twos and breathing the air. But you're not about to push your luck too far this time, not at the risk of being busted. You're standing on the ledge now at the back end of the room, behind all those sitting at the conference table. But almost exactly in front of the direct gaze of the king. There has got to be a better place than this for you to be in. The king might be a bit distraught and distracted now, but who knows when he might momentarily revert to his customary sharp senses and wit and discover an intruder among them? Can't risk that, we've got to find a better spot. Oh, look, there it is, that upright column over there just behind the conference table with the drapery hanging alongside it seems perfect. This will block the view towards you from the king's position, you bet. Unless one of the guests gets up and steps away from the business at hand, and then comes over and deliberately peers through the window by shifting the drapery even, you should be okay. While those at the table seemed well caught up in the matter at hand, nobody seemed likely to be going anywhere anytime soon. Getting over there is going to be a real challenge, though. But you're game too. You're up to this and any other such challenge. So now, after having bided your time very carefully, you've managed to make it there behind the column. You're undercover, yes, but you're having trouble hearing as clearly as you would have liked. Some high-pitched voices sometimes get carried through clearly enough for you to hear what was said. But for the most part, the words are coming through to you (somewhat) muffled. However, left with little, if any other, choices, this will have to suffice, Sis, and then. Listen, there it is. The overture of the haunting melody. Just like the footsteps, the sound is coming. Musical sounds mingled with heavy boots coming. Coming across the floor towards you. Those at the table are still talking; they are all heads, ears, and noses deep into the discussions. But the marching boots type of footsteps are still coming towards you. Even if it's not what you think it is, there's no way you're going to risk finding that out. Speaking of "out," that's what you'll have to do. You'll have to get out of there, out of that place where you are standing now. Or out of sight in any way possible, but out you must get, somehow, and that's what you did. Sliding down on both hands and knees, quickly, very quickly indeed. You swung yourself onto the underside of the ledge on which you had been standing moments before (while wishing for the appearance of the door). Dragging your hands along with you as fast as you possibly could. Whilst stretching out to your fullest length to remain concealed and out of view. Your feet were to have found the column to the southern end in the same way as your hands did, and soft too, as soft as a tomcat hopping across the rocks to go a-fishing for you, perhaps, just as quickly as you had dragged those arms off the ledge above you and out of sight of the guard who had just popped the window open. Just that quickly, you flipped over and popped them across your head to meet the other column on the north side of the building. So now, you're hanging suspended there just below them on the underside of the ledge you had been standing moments before. While thanking the gods for these things and more. First and foremost, the gods you'd long known to be good, before any other. But then, you started having trouble remembering any time or situation in which such gods had ever come through this decisively, quickly, and forcefully for you. Or for anyone you have ever known. So you thought to yourself, it must have been the other gods, the Cekko gods, perhaps, it must have been them who had done it for you. It has got to be the Cekko Gods themselves who have come to your rescue. Yes, you had even started to notice that the strength you would need to bear you up in that position under the ledge was supplied. Even in abundance, it would have seemed, and then, you had to think about sending out some of the praises unto those gods. To magnify those very Cekko gods, too. Maybe, just maybe, you had quickly transcended into becoming much more of a Cekko type of person than you'd thought at first. So you offered up another prayer of thanksgiving unto them, out of the purse. Thanking them for the help they'd provided, and for keeping you there in that position until you could make it down and out of there. Before the hard ground, four stories down came up rapidly to meet you, where you were hanging unprepared and unable to do anything about the situation, any time soon.

Meanwhile, at least one other pair of boots would have marched over to that side of the conference room and might have been there bearing up a second head that's probably there, even now leaning out of the window. A pair of inquiring eyes, too, might be there peering out of the same window and looking around. Searching to see whatever might be there for them to see of any person who might have been loitering around those parts, even you. But then, that was when you began to think the other thoughts. It would have appeared as if it were a superpack supply of strength that the gods had given you for the task, because even after all those many nights and days, while the meeting continued. You were hanging there on the underside of the ledge. Although some passersby would have turned their heads upwards to look in that general direction, and even though you could have seen them clearly as they did so. Somehow, none of them seemed to have even noticed that you were hanging suspended there all that time. Wow! Awesome gods are those.

Chapter 2: Who Will Go?

The chosen one, King Liam, along with his chief ministers, the rangers, and councilors, too, had gotten themselves together to decide on a plan of action. They sent out an agent in keeping with the trail theme that was long established in the Cekko kingdom and the realms of the great kings.

This agent's job was to go, seek, and find the Genode pellets and see to the safe return of those said Genodes back home to the kingdom. These were not just any old Genode pellets, you know, they were real gems. Those that pertain to the kings, and they only. All the Cekko kings, without exception. Those were the very same Genodes pellets that were said to have been stolen from the palace and taken away from the kingdom in a savage revolt staged by Cespedoran, "The vile one," and his cronies. Well, so the story goes on the stone ends. As that story was to go over there on those Cekkolands shores, Cespedoran "The vile one" had grabbed the Genode pellets and run out the doors. Leaving the kingdom and all the ensuing problems behind him, near the fan, with the king's guards in hot pursuit behind them. Along with a bunch of leather-clad warrior women riding on zebra-striped beasts and trailing him and them, to try and reel them back in. To come back home to face up to the truth again. However, there was another version of the story in some spheres over there. Another version of the story has it this way: Cespedoran and his cronies didn't run at all. But they would have fallen through a crack in the flooring wall that had opened up beneath their feet as quickly as a wink of an over-excited Cekko eyelid from the fall. Like, falling and fast-rising up again like your own eyelids that were busily looking at them, same as I did, my friend, you know. Cespedoran and the whole bunch of them would have fallen through the crack that had opened up beneath them before they knew what had hit them. That was then, though, but this is now, no? "Yes."

"I know." This is the present age, and it has been some sixteen thousand years since those occurrences. One agent after another would have been at work. Traveling the world, traversing through time, space, and several dispensations to find and return the lost Genodes, home, in this case. Among other things, tailoring such schemes to get them back home to the kingdom and the throne, and into the proper place beside him to sit down. These Genode pellets were sent down through time and space. On through to modern-day people by the Cespedoran event, as they'd said. They were scattered and sent down, even to people of the humanoid kind. The earthling races, as they are known, yes, by those from ancient times. These pellets must be returned to the palace so that the king's son, his firstborn and only son (or at least, the rightful royal son) and heir to the throne (to be specific) since there may yet be many more sons by the time you get to the "done part" with reading this story in parchment ore, as we did. But whatever the case. The pellets must be returned home to the throne so that this son may live again and reign. We used the words "live again" advisedly here because technically speaking? He's still alive but in a vastly altered state. A state that is not conducive to life in Cekkoland at any level, let alone to have him sitting on the Cekko throne, in disgrace. However, he needs to be restored to optimal health and wellness to continue in the Cekko legacy as it pertains to the kings. The legacy of never-ending life, as it is said of the Cekko kings and the knights. Whether or not it's in Cekkoland, he must, and shall continue to live. Even though he, Bauctnumboulei, unlike how things are with you and me in the current scheme of things in the doorway, may not get to reign in the realms of the great Kings of Cekkoland as he should. Shadow will go, whether he wants to or not.

Shadow Needleman is an agent, well-abled and trusted by King Liam and all his other mighty men, too. It was for this very reason that he was chosen over you, apart from the fact that he liked the guy. The king liked him, that Shadow man (thing), yes, that's why, him. Smokey... yes, Smokey liked him too, it would have seemed. This same Shadow was the first to be entrusted with the task of finding and returning the Genodes home. But not on his own easy-handed will was he drawn into the deal. He was drugged and dragged out of the fields. But then, he would have side-stepped his royal duties and would have been found wandering around and making himself busy dancing with Spooky. He'd even gone so far as to be found messing around with the humanoid kinds and interacting too intimately with them and other such entities along the way. All in his efforts at accomplishing the task, and fulfilling the errands of the day, since you'd asked. Including, but not limited to, interacting with those of the humanoid kind as if he were one of them. Getting drawn way too deeply into them and their ways. All in his quest to get the job done, as it was told to us in those days back home, or was it? The mission was interrupted in the strangest of ways possible. Well, strange that is, if you, just like the Shadow man, would have happened to be out-of-this-world crazy, like me, and not of the humanoid world. But then you'd happen to fall head over heels in love with a dame (or a bunch of them). Dames of the very same humanoid kind, by any given name. Think you've got trouble? Wait until you've got trouble, you'll see. Speaking of having trouble, that Shadow man right there, look at him through the lens of this thing. "See?" "Yes." Yes, as of now, he has surely got that a-plenty. The "trouble" thing? Yes. Even to spare, not running on empty anymore. Shadow would have gotten himself bitten, stupefied by the beauty and charm of an earthling worm, and then another, and yet others, until... Got drawn in by their pretty looks and blinking eye deals. He was "in" so deeply that he almost lost the desire to return to Cekkoland. Well, he did lose the desire, but...

Chapter 3: Got to Go Back to Work

Here comes Smokey, and in the same motion, look, there goes the Ranger. That two-faced son of a lunisun. Sliding just like the eel, he has quickly become since heading up the defense portfolio and rolling the wooden spoon. There he goes, sliding out of Shadow's sleeping chamber after having gone in and administering the potion onto the pillow where Shad will be planting his weary head in a New York minute's time. Then drifting away into Slumber-land, from which he won't be returning any time soon to view the sunshine, but he doesn't know. Shad doesn't know any of that yet. Smokey would have made sure that it would be so. He was careful to make sure of that, among other things, while on the go to stir the pot, you know. He... the Smokey being. It was that said Smokey dude who would have worked it all in on him, probably by way of his plate of food and commitment to sin. He also made sure, while he was at it, to furnish the long-term form of Cekkolandee fix, so that he wouldn't be coming back any time soon to sit. Smokey was the first to quit the conference room, uncharacteristically so, and said he had a few minor chores to get done while he could still keep his eyes open. And while his feet were still on the go, those things could not wait, so he'd said. Shadow, in the meantime, was having no end of trouble keeping his own eyes open to look at you and to view the sunshine. He blinked rapidly as he reached out to take a strong-arm hold of the doorknob and pull the door open. Out of the corner of his eyes, he could have sworn that he saw something move. He hesitated just long enough to convince himself that it was nothing, nothing at all. He needed to get some shut-eye and fast.

Meanwhile, look down at the far end of the hall. Somebody who looked a lot like Smokey to Shadow's sleepy eyes, who could barely see anything anymore, turned the corner so very fast that he would have scraped his shoulder on the 90-degree edge of the wall in the process. While holding the hem of the black housecoat he was wearing and pulling it in front of the fast-running away legs. He wrapped the coat around him and hoped the action would save him precious split seconds, enough for him to get out and stay out of sight. Not to be found out and to be busted, no, not on this night. He cannot afford another setback, not now. He was lucky, it would have seemed, enough to get out of there and not be seen. He then headed down to the closest staircase; down into the servants' quarters of the building, where his son should be (by then) fast asleep in his tiny sleeping chamber, tucked away in the farthest northern corner of the building, and underground. He spoke the code upon nearing the cubicle. The door swung open to let him slide in and push it back close behind him fast, and leaving you out there in the dark, no? "No." "Well, if you say so, Dell."

Smokey is the Chief Ranger, the chief agent in charge there. He has free access to almost any chamber in the building and most other facilities on the compound, I hear. Meaning, he'll have no trouble at all getting around. So, there he goes into the rooming house, or so I'd supposed. The young boy stirred to life on the father's entry into the chamber, happy to see his father again, as usual. They exchanged pleasant words and hugs as they embraced, disturbing the bugs in the place. He embraced the son's face again before the father tucked the son back in under the warm night covering cloth. Look! He's rubbing the head of the young boy, ruffling the low-cut brown hair somewhat before turning around and then walking back to the exit door. The same way by which he'd come before. Look at him there, he stopped in the doorway and leaned in.

"You know I love you, don't you?" he said. The boy nodded and shook his head in agreement, while pulling the covering cloth back up under the chin with a grip from both hands. Smokey's neck and head popped back on the inside as he nodded again and winked approvingly at the young boy on his final exit out of the chamber, waving a fan to cool himself down. While pulling the door shut behind him, well, as far as I can remember, that's how these things happened. Smoking Smokey has one more thing to see about before he calls it quits for the night, and goes out to get some food and shut-eye before we get to daylight.

Look, Smokey is now in the lab. It's his domain, so there is nothing to it, you might think, on a hiss and sob, if one should have happened to be somewhere around, though, somewhere close enough to sneak a peek at him on a drive through Benbow. Like, peeking through a crack in the door, or through a curtain, perhaps. Or by way of something else, you know, like, by way of any and everything with see-through cracks. Such a person would've been likely to see a somewhat altered Smokey. Altered from the norm was he, because... Look at him. He's apprehensive now; there's an air of uneasiness about him this time. His physical demeanor is noticeably out of whack. Off-beat, he is walking the line somewhat. But, he's there. Look, look at him through the lens of this thing. There he is, pouring essence from one vial after another, carefully selected fragrances, too, and chopped spices. He's pouring it all into the glass tube, and then into the bubbling pot over the fiery flame, as may be determined by the master brewer himself; he sure has a name. He's stirring the pot now with one spoon-equipped hand and shaking the glass tube with the other. Rapidly now. Look, he's applying drops of the liquefied mix from the tube into the pot periodically, and the spices, too, as he shakes and stirs yet more. Look at him there! Looking back at who? Probably you, beware! Not seeing you behind the door there yet, though. There you are in that tiny spot with the leaned-up chair, no? "No." "Yes, a makeshift brace it is, drawn over and placed behind the door to bar you in and all the others out of the crib. Including him, Smokey, by the Shadow Man, no doubt." The pot is boiling in Smokey's kitchen and bubbling under his hand. As clouds of steam mushroom up from the belly of the boiling pot, fogging up the ceiling and curling down the back. He now stops the shaking and the stirring. Look, he's putting down the glass tube, and with his bare-naked hands, he's now holding the pot, and, what the...? Look at that, he's lifting it off the fire and then tilting it sideways to pour out some of the mixture from the pot and into the fire itself. The inferno, oh my! Look, look at the flames as they go up, up, up. The inferno is erupting... "That's amazing!" Unlike how things are with us in the earthly realms, when seen in these and such things, Smokey does not seem perturbed at all. Even though the flame is swinging as if it is clinging to the sleeves of the lab garments he's wearing. Wow! What a dude. Look! He's putting the pot down on a table a little way removed from the fireplace and is walking over to a cupboard. Now, keep on looking, you coward! Did you see that? He's reaching into the cupboard and taking out something. "What is it?" Oh yes, there it is. It's another vial and... but-but, why is he moving so fast with that bottled-up glass and-and, and what's that? Oh! It's a pair of pliers, but why? I can't say for sure, but he's walking back to pour some of the liquid from that vial into the pot. Look at that! A cloud of steam is billowing out of the pot, still. He's fanning the pot now as if to quickly cool it down, and blowing steamy breath from his mouth in through the lips pointed round. He's reaching back into the other cupboard for a bowl of some sort, and a scoop too. Look, he just pulled it out of the drawer, and with it, he's now dishing out some of the potions from the potted brew and into the bowl to fill it up to overfill with the broth, to come over and give it to you as a start, no? "No." Oh well, if you say so, what can I do? But still, keep on looking, look at him go. He picks up the bowl and is now walking. Walking towards the door, left half-open. Still walking. He's walking out of the lab now and going down the corridor. Down the stairs, he is now going towards the sleeping chambers where he had been earlier to hide with her. Look at him, he's going towards the door of the chamber again and entering the chamber where he knows he's sleeping, along with the rest of them. All of them, like his helpers and associates, are there each evening, including him. "Yes?"

"Yes, including his son." Smokey's son, Sparks, was a top-level secret in the kingdom. "It was a business deal," so they say, when everything was said and done. He never wanted it to become a certified regular right away, "he just wanted one of those things," like a son. I guess he had hopes, dreams, and plans, one might say. Big plans, it would seem; big plans for the future, and for realizing his dreams of the day. The agreement with the chambermaid was signed, sealed, and delivered. Both sides were satisfied, so she bore him a son. He then sent her off to be married to, or as the terms were for that sort of thing in Cekkoland, certified regular. They were to then certify it as "regular" by doing those sorts of Cekko things irregularly, until it was done. So, the popular story went on to say, she would become a "Certified regular." She was assigned to a distant relative of his and would be afforded a rare chance to live out the rest of her very long life, lived according to Cekkoland's standards of the kings and the knights. But as for her? As of this point, it will come with grandeur and flair off Smokey's arm. Well, again, so the story goes over there, but then, be forewarned. Not quite unlike how it is with the kings and their consorts, but there are some small differences here, of sorts. The difference, as it goes in the case of the kings, was like this, as it applies to women in these sorts of setups and things. Any Cekko woman would much rather sign on the dotted line with someone who was anything like Smokey or any of the men under him, smartly. More so than they would have been with the king, be it the current king, King Liam, or any other king throughout the ages. The reason for this is that... Unlike how it was to go with this arrangement between them and Smokey (Sparky's pops), where the woman in question was to have gone on to live a full and somewhat respectable life by way of the swaps. When it comes to the Cekko kings, such a woman can never go on to establish a new relationship with other men. Let alone certify it as "regular" with them. In other words, to regularize it in marriage as such things are referred to in the humanoid world in the earthly realms, and on the humanoid carriage, to get it to them. At least, that is how it works in theory with them. Many are the stories, though, popular stories such as those told to us in the days of glory on Cekko ore. Stories of babies being born to these very sorts of women, and then being done away with, in one form or another. There were many other stories, too, of babies being laid away, encased in storage chambers under the Royal Housing Complex with you. Indoors, too, if I remember well how these things were said to be true, no? "No." "Okay." Some of them were alive, even, because they would not die, no matter how hard some people were known to have tried. Spooky. Spooky indeed are those babies. Babies whose eyes (up until then) had never seen the lights of a Cekko sunrise. Or even a sunset, for that matter, that's such a surprise. But a day is coming, and it's just about here, when some long-hidden things, secrets even, will be made known. Things will be revealed soon. Every eye shall behold it. Everyone's eyes in Cekkoland are now watching, and all are waiting for the fallout. Oh sheet! Look at this.

Chapter 4: Waking Up There in the Shadow of Trees

There was nothing to it; it was as ordinary a day as any. Shadow was there, feeling a bit peckish, I hear. Yes, hungry he was. He had not eaten anything in weeks and was beginning to feel a bit weak. He reached into the shoulder sack and fished out from there, one of the silver nuggets. Travel food to nibble on and grub it. Silver nuggets and water are all that is needed for his sustenance on the journey, on the far side; if all else fails, he always has a prayer. A never-failing, ever-dependable prayer. One can never go wrong with that, right?

"Right."

"You liar."

So, he sat down at the base of a large oak tree just a few giant steps away from the water's edge, and me, I mean, I... As he reached into the side bag hanging from his shoulder, bare and cried, "Help me." Then, he reached in deeper with his right hand and begged. He begged for it and just as quickly received it from the keg when he would have fished out one serving of the very well-preserved meal. He then nibbled away on the silver nugget until it was all done, as is the norm. Or until he had his fill, until he was full of it, you know. "I must not drink water while I'm eating my nugget," he grunted repeatedly and spat on it. He has always had to verbally remind himself of that small detail. Otherwise, he runs the risk of forgetting and breaching that code. If he does, he will also be found to be there breaching the overload and going on to sleep away for years in humanoid terms and time measures down the road, as such things were found, written in the codes of the ages. The Shadow Man doesn't have that kind of luxury, no. There's a job to be done; ways yet for him to go, and it has waited way too long already as it is, no? "Yes."

Having finished feasting on the silver nugget, and yet again. After waiting until the sun had gone around in a circle, one dark and one light. Up to and around the same point where it was in the skies when he had his meal that night. He can then have as much water to drink as he may need on this earth. The Earth, where humanoids live and work, I think! So, down into the water, he went and go... from his perch up there at the base of the old oak tree, you know? Look, that giant oak tree standing right there, proud and boasting on the riverbank, across from me, here giving thanks. Can you not see it? "Yes, that one right there." It was there that he sat down and feasted, among the many other things that are documented and well-known that he did. Many are the other things he would have done there in that square, eventually. But, as of now? Look, he's stooping. He stooped down by the water's edge and scooped up handful after handful of refreshingly cool, clear water. Took it to his dry, thirsty lips and sucked it in thereafter. But then, at about the halfway point through the routine. He heard it and turned around to look and to inquire, I mean. To the right of him, he saw it. There he was, someone was sitting there in a canoe amongst the bugs. Just sitting there watching him and slapping them with his... ugh. While looking back and forth between him and you. No? "No." Of course, it was happening, like so. He didn't know who it was or what it was about at the time. He had never seen anyone quite like him before dining on his dinner thyme. He only knew that; this time, a being was there. Of that, he was quite sure to be fair. There he was, a being of some kind, it looked like some kind of human, sitting there and doing something. Like, busy with his hands working against the bugs' sting. Some of the humanoid kind of beings, doing what humanoids do, perhaps. He wasn't quite sure about much, but he knew enough about that; he was there. The being was there and sitting on some sort of contraption that floated on top of the water. Not on-air as is the custom over there on the far side, so I hear, mi pastor. This humanoid-looking kind of being was watching him very attentively. But at the same time, he was doing other things to try and frighten me (out of my mind). Shadow was trying to communicate with the being in the usual and customary way. Firstly, by a wave of the hand and then a bow of the head like... like this, eh. But he did not respond. At least not in a like manner as it was said and done. He spoke, though, in a strange sort of "other" language, like so. Shadow talked back at him in proper Cekko language, of course, the king's own Cekko language, no doubt. Everybody knows and speaks it, right? But not Man-ho-Manuel, not on this night. He just sat there and stared at him in wonder. "What the hell..." Shad was wondering what it all meant. He would eventually make beckoning gestures towards Shad, though, which he'd interpreted as a call to action of some sort (or not). A call to join him on board the floating contraption to go, well, perhaps. "Not in your life," said the Shadow man to him that same night. Again, in a language only known to him in and around these parts on the bend, so it would seem. "There's no way I'm getting in that thing with you," he said, upon the back-and-forth shaking of the head. They're out in the deep waters now and sailing ahead. The boat ride is cool, too, after all, Shad is even getting into the finer aspects of the fishing thing to call. He would have caught quite a few fish himself by the time they were all done. They had enough food to feed the family and to boil the pots (or none). So the road now leads back home. Or, to the safe side of town over on the other shore near the pearly rocks, as they are known. Where they can begin to bond man-to-man, or man to... "Whatever." Yeah! That one. No. Don't be clever. Just come along, look... They're roasting fish on a coal fire by the water's edge and eating their fill of it, and then, look. Man-ho, or Manuel, as he would from then on begin and come to be known to the Shadow Man. Manuel, the fisherman, got the bright idea to take it all the way home. Back to the place where he and the rest of his clan live, and calls it all his home. Way out there in a floating village across the deep. Across many deep and shallow waters, too, so to speak. So, onward home, the ship then sails back to you. No?

Chapter 5: Close Encounter of the Feminine Kinds

There were other times, too, like when the Shadow man was to meet up with some humanoid types of women. Hear from him now, as he went on to tell us a little bit about that and other such scores, in his own words, he meant.

The earthlings sometimes spoke of a place, a wonderfully blissful place. "Heaven," they call it, or some such thing like that, with prophets. "It makes me want to go there," he said, sometime in the future, perhaps. Well, at least once before I return to my place, far away from these beautiful babies, and back to my rightful place among the Cekko kings in the KD's. "It's not half bad out there," they say. I tend to agree with that too today. It was like, like. It was like this. She was the first of many women I met there, amongst those of the humanoid kind. Boy! It was like I was cursed from ancient times. Lying there with her like that for the first time, all the pain I never knew I could feel happened, and I found myself wanting to immerse myself in her, often. You know, like, into all of her, all the time. But I never knew how until she would enlighten me. At her touch, all the pain disappeared like a whisper from the guts, as I was to hear it and see. Is this what they mean whenever they speak so glowingly of "heaven"? I wondered about these and swore at them. It's got to be! After those things, we started treading more cautiously like, just in case. But there was to be no more stopping us from running the race. Or even from taking vows, in those days. We would lie beside each other, you know, like, like always, and then it happened. Again, and again. We lie next to each other a lot less now. Well, not now-now, you know. But, now as in, you know what I mean, I mean, eventually. Eventually, we drifted apart, seeing each other less… and less of each other. Then came the departure of both of us from all of that sort of disorder. That thing tends to do that to people you know. While it lasted, though, we were enabled. Two hearts beating as one right here, above the navel, but, lightly, we were touched sometimes when every part of this old man's being wants to be doing more. Much more than just that. It was a thin line. That's as unnatural and nerve-racking a thing as there is. But it was, it was as, as, it was as if I was falling apart, man, at the seams. Bit by bit, as in dreams, and then… It didn't just happen out of the blue, you know. She would have grown on me, and tried as I may, I could not break away. I found her there that night, slumbering beneath a spiky finger of moonlight under the canopy of the tall old oak trees in the forest where… I swear. Long I sat there and watched her, while in dreams she slept. But then she stirred to life, eyes wide open and wet. Look, she's now staring at me, as if she liked what she was seeing, or did she? Her hair began springing to attention on the nape of her neck. Erectile tissue then stirred unbidden beneath the epidermis of a stranger in the night. "What, what the heck!" I was sweating, soaking wet. Abruptly, she sat up, looking at me through the waking cup. Her eyes had an inner fire, a boldness that reasoned in sync with me from some hidden places deep within, oh! The desire welled up from within me and pulled on the wire. Those voices were communicating with me, and me with them, and her, speaking to her senses it would seem, or with her innate responses to danger, even in her dreams. Stimulating a resolve to fight, probably. Or to take the flight off me. She can take on the biggest of threats and promptly defeat them, you know. She was going to, yes, she was going to fight, I was sure of that. But I was not the least afraid, because — "Because of what?"

"Because those qualities did inspire and stir me deeply within my braids, that's what." Until she pounced on me like a gazelle, knocking me out cold as... well. Before I knew what it was that had hit me, way back to the fold. Or so she thought, it would seem. Maybe that's how it works in the humanoid world and her dreams. But as for me? The violent whack did serve the useful purpose of jolting me back to some semblance of reality. Got my eyes focused again and got myself to see. I came up striking back in a normal self-preserving way. "You can't walk one country mile in my footwork," I said to her, before getting back to hitting the score. Not remembering or even caring one iota about that and other things to save the day's quota, of a bore. You know, like, that she was one of those from the "opposite way". A sexy thing to say. Which got me started referring to her as something like "sex," or some other such object. "A woman," they say, as opposed to a manly way. That's what they call her out there, I think. This got me really vexed, even to a stink. I smacked her hard upside the head in the very next wink. She went flying, headfirst, into the trunk of the nearby Oak, I think, happened before I even spoke, or sank to my knees. But, oh please! Look at these! I heard voices whispering through the trees. She was a much fiercer fighter than I thought when at first she would have spoken, of the sort. She came back kicking like a mule and biting like a crocodile. And then. Up from the ground where she had landed fell, yes, fallen with my next best punch. Sobbing in a low tone and crawling back at me to take the rest of the lunch. She came up with a knife and cut off a piece of my ear. Don't forget to thank that Johnny fellow over there for this pint of beer, alright? "Alright." So. After bouts of fighting all night. I ended up moments later making peace with her from a prostrate position under a large oak tree. Gosh, oh, how I loved that woman. The best one for me, well, among the many, you know! Such as this one.

They usually come in twos and threes, you know. So, Shadow was running low on the silver nuggets again. They'd done well to sustain him over the centuries, up until then. But more than anything else, he wanted a change. After all, he'd been away from the place he'd come to know and called his home for quite a long time, and was here interacting with these other beings. Trying his best to start blending in a little more with them, it would have seemed. Well, maybe it was that, and maybe he also wanted to start partaking even more in some of their customs, rituals, and traditions from around those parts. He went out once again with the chief on the next fishing trip. It was another of the chief's regular deep-sea fishing escapades down into it, way down into the deep belly of the sea. See? "Yes." Okay then, look at me. "This is where the big games are," he was told. This is where you want to be. Down there, it's not too cold. Just below the floating village community on the surface square is where the chosen community divers of the year would go and collect the periodic supplies, he was told. Yes. "There, in front of your eyes, guys," I swear! That's what I hear. But he must have lied, because. "Here's the drill," said the new chief to him. In an attempt at preparing him for the trip down under — "Under his skin, right?"

"No, not under his skin, ma-hite, but under the village in those parts and partings." He then went on to explain it to him in great detail. All of the "dos and don'ts" that the task would entail. He went about schooling the Shad. So, the deal, as it turned out, was for him to prepare his mind and body, lungs and all. Prepare for the long trip down into the belly of the deep; headlong, he went into the fall. To go and get the fish up from down there and bring them up to the surface, where the family should be waiting for dinner. All that food to eat and share to feed them all. All that has got to be done with just one breath of fresh air within her and him. "No problem, mate. Nothing to win." "Oh no, wait, my dear," she said to him. There's much more for you to see and hear, hmm-muah. "Now swim," she said, after giving it to him near his head. Shad was confident, and boy! He sure was buoyed. After all, this is the shadow, this is Shadow Needleman whom you are talking to here. I've done some real out-of-this-world sorts of things in my life and timing. Things that will make your skull pop-kaboom just like that, and winding, just to think of it. This swimming, diving, and fishing bit, of which you now speak. This, too, will be just another notch on my pistol shot of the week. So he said to all of them, and to this little gal, so to speak, his friend. Oh! Look at her, isn't she sweet? "No."

"Well! Let's go get some fish to eat, or sell," said the chief to this inky elk. Yes, that will be all, go on now, tell, or else you'll fall to the sword, anyway, just leave, because... How wrong could the Shadow Man have been? But then again, how could he even have known these things, that this was his last ride home and in? As in, that said, sleeping gown skin? Two sleeps later, they were up and ready to go, leaving behind the boring old hater... and that was when they hopped out and through the gated door. Out on the deck, they got up and went, after briefly reworking their routines, again. Then they took the plunge down, down, down. The tightness in his chest was getting stiff, and stiffer still, like this thing here. Cliffy, the chief, was ready to do it, just like Manuel had done in another world among the thieves. In another place and time, and another depth. Another deep watery pearl, like these girls of thine, yes. The chief beckoned him onward, forward, and deeper down. "You will then hit the transition point," the chief had said while rolling the joint, before sitting back down against the bed that night, on a rather sharp point. But the only transition that Shad could see coming for him was his chest bursting open and sucking salty seawater rushing in. Bracing and grating hard at the inner walls of his lungs where fresh air so longed to be to begin, like, with, yes, in there. It felt like water was getting into the air space there and drowning him. It must have happened just like that, at that very moment in fact, because that's the last thing he remembered of that fishing expedition. Furthermore, that was, and still is, the only other "black-out" spot in the many lives of the Shadow man that he could not and still cannot quite get clarity on from anyone. Nor is he able to figure it out on his own, Cekko's plan. As to what might have happened there and then. After that fateful moment, and on, the questions keep piling up in the tin can. Questions as to what might have happened there and then? Like: Did he die there, as is the custom with those of the humanoid kind, over here? If so, if he'd died that time. Did he forfeit another of his many lives there? The humanoid inserts of what he was given as "life" to equip him for the humanoid world on this earthling's side, over here? Was he rescued from that situation? If so, by whom? How long was he out of it? On and on, the question kept piling up within the pan and gnawing at him. They were just supposed to go out for a swim, and then some more. He sold Shad on the idea, and, swimming, he went with him off the shores of Arcadia in the deep. That was the last he ever saw or heard of the chief, the villagers. Or Man-ho-Manuel again, he thinks. What had happened? He may never know for sure. But he was quite sure that he'd woken up in jail. Walking the yards, surrounded by a battalion of strange soldiers and guards. Lugging around the pail, life as he knew it was never the same again. Oh hell! Then comes his fear of everything to do with the world of water and fishing. In the realms of the great kings in Cekkoland, where Shadow came from. It's two strikes over there, and you're out and gone. Unlike what seems to be a custom here in the humanoid realms, where it takes all of three. No doubt, Shad is not going to risk a third from anybody. Even if he's to be given another chance at doing so, so I've heard. Even if it's in the humanoid world that he's to be found living at the time. He's not going to risk it, not on yet another of the many chances of losing his dime on viewing Netflix. Not on his life over here on this earthling's side of the holey biscuit. Now, though, the Shadow Man has got one more thing to worry about. Yet another thing to fear here in the humanoid world as he went about his task, seeking to find and return the lost Genodes' home. To add to his fear of sleep, the fear of water, and the deepest parts there, there is now an additional worry, constantly gnawing at the Shadow man and his psyche... Curry, go to sleep.

Chapter 6: The Coming of the "Sisters" Kinds

The men there, they say, are from Mars and the women are from Venus, okay? Meanwhile, divorces and breakups skyrocketed one day, way up. That's over there, though, not here, I'm sure. "Or is it the other way around, the shore to show us more?" Now, go. Get away from here before... No, wait, not yet, not until you hear this.

Shad found himself again caught up in a crack. He was to be found caught up again in a similar situation to that. It seems to be becoming "a thing" happening all too much, and too often to him. He wanted that woman so very badly that... But the other woman wanted him too and was making it known to all of them, gladly. "Shiue!" She was not leaving anything up to mere chances, and you. So, because of the urgency, he had to hurry to get to the place that intersects Cornwall and Surrey. Yeah! In your face, it's still blurry, but don't worry; don't go rushing it. No need over here for the powdered curry, oh sheet! Hear this. Now, here's the story, listen to it while you eat the dory, fish ee.

While Sharone was there, busily soaking up his attention. The other women in the room were busily acting out the sideshow on the ascension. Hertha nodded in insight and received Tamara's insightful whispered wisdom along with the garment she had carefully folded and given. Handed off to her, in her thoughtful and melodious humming heaven, as it occurred. She knew how it was going to end with those two. The two of them could be nothing more than just friends who are just the normal ones like me and you. Just like always, she wasn't holding back on the reminders. The anecdotes were used to support her theories from all those days behind her. They were insightful bits and pieces of information, advice, and instructions as to what they all needed to do there and therein that night. To ensure the proper outcome, the one that's right, fair, and best for all concerned, there. Their next moves were precisely crafted—"Why, but, but, why?"

"They needed to get a grip on the situation fast, kid. That's why." To keep their heads screwed on the right, you know, because... As you already know, somebody has got to keep their head on while everywhere else, everyone else seems to be losing theirs slowly, yes, that slow, Leigh, right? "Right." You know, they knew very well that that "somebody" around those parts was Tamara. "That's who?" Yes, Tamara was that somebody in and around those parts, it would seem, even to him, and at that particular moment, no better person could have been found for the task than Tamara on the home end, not in your dreams. Those other women were there, but acting disinterested and indifferent. As Tandi grew more upset, though, her inner thoughts and disgust began to show. Her well-trained hands were briskly turning out, flagging out, and then folding up the garments to dispel the excess heat. Along with her hard hand swiping to render them smooth and neat. Those acts, too, were becoming, likewise, increasingly more precise. "True, almost perfect, right?"

"Yes, almost like fried rice. Look! Isn't it nice?"

"Yes, it is nice when done right, but..."

Look. Everything is sharp and crisp now, until one could almost cut and shave Grandpa's silvery beard under his brow. With the razor-sharp edges of the fabric, that is, the folded fabrics, that's how. No, not with the machete, not the sow, none of that, just this, and even more so than these. It could surely cut through the tension in the laundry room, but it did not; nothing did, in fact. Shadow was, (in the meantime) shaking, visibly at the knees, evenly, and aching. Unlike how it was waiting to go along the road, with Steven, he wasn't going to be leaving. At least not yet. Not before he gets what he's out there to get. Whatever confidence he once had in his ability to maintain his composure in all situations, though. Was, as of this point, a withered thing, limp and hanging low, nearly dead on the vine near the bough, we think. He'd met his match, somehow, and what was he supposed to do about that? Blow-wow! He couldn't quite see. There were other women there, too. After all, this is their domain to go do what they often do, or to come to call and get me through. It's a place where they go to do the things that they are prone to do over there, among you, a laundromat and all. But these six had a vested interest in all this. Had to dictate and direct the outcome of the matter at hand, seemingly. Whatever the motive, really. Be it personally or protectively, the interest was there effectively. Ava had scampered just like a frightened mouse out of the room. Large, the fluffy grey cat must have loomed. She was seen quitting the steamy place just as steaming mad as the sizzling, steamy wet pad. But as for Tseshie? See what she sees? Look, Tseshie would have made a more dignified and leisurely departure out the door. Dragging her reluctant feet under her some more. You know, dragging them along under her plumb and fine swaying frame. Waiting for someone with a noble name, like Tamara, for instance, or Hertha. Or any of the others. She was slow-walking and waiting for them to pitch in and hurt her just a bit further. Her friends, even. Or for anyone else who'd be found interested enough to come and rescue her from her reluctant departure, leaving to go outback, through the fast door. To call her back and apologize, in fact, for spoiling their laundry day meet-up and chit-chats, not very nice doing that, no. For stirring things up when and where they had no business stirring anything, not even that one, for him, and upsetting her by doing so. But that never happened; that apology never came. Though she was walking slowly, dragging her feet heels-and-toe, Leigh. Waiting for it, probably. Nothing was going to be the same from that moment on, though she knew it darn well. They all knew it too and could tell, but then. What in Cekko heaven's name was Shadow supposed to do about those two when next they were to meet up again, over stew? Shad couldn't help but notice, theirs were the two sternest faces in those places. There, in a sea of other disapprovingly stern and thinning feminine brows, for as short a while as it had been. Look at them. Wow! As for Tamara and the other women, like Hertha. Those two were left with the task of seeing to the well-being of their bossy friend, Sharone. From there on and on the way home to get homey, and telephoning the dome man while at home with you and me, no? "No." Those two add more heat to the old bones, though. His bones, even. At least one of them did, as it was told to me and the kids. As for Shad, though inexperienced, he might have been in such earthly things to have. He knew enough to have known that trouble was brewing; those were two innately opposite types of women to him. He loved and wanted both of them. "Nothing but trouble can come from this," he knew it, suited him just fine. "Screw it."

But how did the Shadow man come to fall so hard upon this? How did he get here, behind this pint of beer? Let's go back to where it was said to have all gotten started, back to a bed-chamber somewhere over there in Cekkoland on the star grid. Shad plunked himself down rather heavily on the sleeping sack in the sleep chamber, as much as he's able to tell us and remember. He then heaved his left leg up and out of the sandals. Cross-hitched left ankle atop his right knee. Then brushed the sole of his foot with his right hand quickly, like me. Back, forth, and then back again a couple of times with sharp, purposeful strokes. He then turned his attention to the other leg in a similar manner. Then proceeded to administer the same tender treatment as before, before he would have been a goner. He leaned to one side behind the door. After pulling the feet up onto the sleeping place, some more, he pulled the covering cloth over his head and face and was almost instantaneously out of it, fast asleep. The beginning of thousands of years of sleep and slumbering, he didn't foresee. Let alone planned for, behind the sorcerer's door key. When the shadow man woke up next. He was in the other realm of another World Cup, vexed, and wondering what in the name of Cekkolords had hit him. Not to worry, though, Shad. You'll have all the time in the world that you may need, to have. Your world, the one back home, even, but the new ones also. New to you only because you had just arrived here, and yes, there too. But as a "just comer coming to her on the Newlands," but new anyway, anyhow. In all of the schemes of Cekko things, even the moo-cow and fatted cock chickens. You will have plenty of time. All of the time, you may need, in fact, to figure it all out and to relax. King Liam and his son, though, Bauctnumboulei, the little kid on the go, Bey. They both need you to be strong and to see this through, okay? But! "What kind of people do things like that?" Shad wondered out loud and reacted sometime later when he was a little bit waker. "What sort of mind would have conceived such a thing?" He wondered from within, again. To have sent a man away, a warrior even. Sent him out on a mission without the benefit of his tried, tested, and proven weapon? But then again. Smokey did send his son out on the road masked as a hopping toad, burdened down heavily to carry the load and all of that code. So there, it could have been someone like him, beware. Someone like that, Smokey being, might have been behind the happening. But not necessarily him. The last time, though, that Shadow Man would have known how anything really, really goes. Or when he would have felt like a soldier. A real Cekko soldier and a warrior. Or even like a real Cekko-type of a man, and not a carry-over. It was on the last night of the last meeting. He had his weapon there in his hand to greet him. Had it all day long, as was the custom, he was ready to slay what at first he'd thought was an intruding one. But he must have been wrong, had been up and working for way too long, yeah, probably that one. Because Shad was quick on the draw. Sword in hand and ready to send it to Taw. The intruder was going to be sent for a stint in a stack pile of straw, on some other strand. Or get sent down to the repair shop, like, damn. The scrapheap of long times to lay him on, or in the assimilation chamber where he'd once stained her. Or maybe he could go all the way and toss him away and further on, like, unto the other scrap heaps for body parts he'd become. But he was really, really beat. Could hardly even stand up firmly on his feet. It didn't take very long for him to pass it all off as a sleep log on. Too much time away from the sheets back home, brought on by lack of rest and meat. The overexposure to the sleeplessness of the long meeting week. In the next Cekko minute or two, he was out of it. Out of the kit and fast asleep like you, still there talking sheet. But we still need to find out what he's talking about. So, can somebody please tell me? Did he go through the chamber? The A-chamber, did he go through there to get him out of there, and on the way? He can't seem to remember how it happened on that day, on the first occasion to get away from there, but he would have wondered. He had no real idea, none whatsoever. But if he were a gambling man, which he's certainly not. Not like I am, but if he should have been asked to place a bet and set it on that. It would have been biased towards the girls carrying him out. In a similar manner, they will soon be carrying Beahon and Angela home against the shouts, to become a goner. You hang around here and wait for the start of those other happenings, coming around the very next corner. You'll see, but you didn't hear it from me, alright? "Alright." He's not sure of that either, one way or the other. He just knew that he would have gone to bed. To bed down in his very own regular bed in his very own regular bed chamber on one very tired and yet tiring night, and was to find himself woken up, however much time later on, in a faraway land with a job to perform, then be gone. But, "gone" he was from that very moment on. Well, up until he was to be mal-handled yet again, and brought back home to relax and sit down with him, eventually. Literally, but not completely. "Sit down, servant." His job is far from done. "Sit down, nuh, servant, relax."

"You know I can't sit down, no, pops."

"Sit on it. Whatever 'it' is. Just sit". (Too darned unruly you are). Note: ((Thought bubble)) of the king is what it is. Come on into the car with the kids.

Chapter 7: Handle with Care

Even after all those years in prison, there was no sign of ever getting out anytime soon. Shadow was still a very impatient being, but was to be there, waving a worry spoon, all around him. His brilliant ideas, though, came about on this basis. "Oh!" While sitting there in prison for all those years, with longing in his eyes and shedding no proud tears. He would have managed to notice that they existed in parallel universes. He and his hosts, that is, the jailers, with the most bratty kids. They all existed in a separate dimension from that of the other creatures who seemed to float by from time to time. He was trapped there, and tried as he may, he could not seem to be able to get away. Oh no, he couldn't get out, kid, no matter how loudly he hollered and shouted. The jailers, though, guards, and other workers alike in the yard could come and go as they liked. In the same way as those in authority everywhere in the universe seemed to do and remain sober all night, and bright like you. But not so with their charge, the prisoner, Shadow Needleman, in this case of the shoe he'd promised and given her, from you, and at your eagerly giving hands, no? "No." However, in another dimension, it would also seem to him like other creatures. In particular, those "other" kinds of reapers, as they are referred to by the jailers and guards over there behind the irons and bars. Or even those of the humanoid forms, as you are, those who were often seen out there walking through the woodlands. They could move around however much they wanted to, so it would have seemed, to the good ones who... Sometimes they would walk right by the camp and its occupants, or even right over them and him if they were not careful to get the hell out of the way on their approach and be gone clean at once, and fast. But no communication seemed to be taking place between those two groups, no talks. But then, once upon one of those times. It so happened that Shadow was out there relaxing, again. He'd gone out walking that morning and then come back in to them, and was to be seen still sitting there on his smooth, shiny rock-turn-chair. The hole in the rock was not only getting deeper as time passed by over there. But it seemed to be taking the shape and form of his hardened backside more and more each year. Don't ask me why, you hear? But as he was sitting there under his shady tree, he heard it. No, not from me, but... oh, sheet! Listen, there it is, that's the same sort of rattling that was heard going on in the forest by his shaky knees, an unusual rattling, like this. Very attentively, Shadow was listening as the rattling sounds were getting closer to you and me. Closer and closer still. Closer and clearer yet, until.... Shadow's eyes, in the meantime, were searching and surveying the courtyard carefully. Very carefully, his eyes were sweeping the surroundings to search for... well, whatever was there to be seen on the reveal to the court's guards, not me. But, tough luck. Nothing was to be found coming up. Well, not about the guards and their reaction cup, but yes, he was busy there, listening in on things and examining the behavior of the guards themselves, trying to see and hear. Did they hear what he had just heard? Maybe not yet. But will they eventually hear it? And what if they do, what will they do next? It took him yet another thirty to forty human years to figure that out and then start formulating and fine-tuning a plan of action. To deal with that, and other such things, was about to become the new customs. Shad had always harbored a nagging fear of losing his precious cargo. He'd toiled long and hard to gain possession of those pellets in the car, though. By using whichever of the tools he would find in his possession at any given time. Or whatever the hell else he could find breaching the lines, mainly the scanners this time. The scanners were what he found there. Two, to be exact. But to be fair, there he was, my pops, in the custody of a brutish prison and its drill sergeants and guards. He, therefore, came crawling hard upon a fabulous plan of action. Designed to protect and preserve the Genode scanner pellets from crooks and any of their interactions, until he would have been able to use them to furnish his fix. He inserted the scanner pellets into the cylinder of his needle pen and then proceeded from then on to keep a king-sized vigil over it. This lasted for the duration of the time while he was there, holed up in the custody of that rotten prison and its several change-of-guards and cadets. The many changes of captains, too, as you might have guessed on the finger licks and chew, yes. This may have amounted to nearly ten thousand earth-years in humanoid terms and time measurements if his memory is to serve him right. Since he's been having a lot of trouble trusting his memory, in recent times, he wouldn't want to go and bet on it this time either, not on this Nightline, meager. But he had always had the protection of his cargo at heart. He was still that smart. He had to be vigilant at all times. He could not afford to lose those kingdom dimes, and losing them wasn't even an issue for him at first. But after what had happened with the fishing mishaps and the curse. He was beginning to think that he must have lost some of the edges off his act, because what else was there to be the reading on that call? How could one, anyone at all? How could anyone explain his present predicament, or even the fall? Nowadays, if there's one thing that he fears, other than the fear of sleeping and never finding the Genode pellets, and losing his scanners to the thieving... in the coming years. It would be the fear of losing his pellets to water, of all things, there and thereafter. The Genodes must be passed on down through the ages by way of the firstborn sons of all of the kings, in the KDs. The royal offspring. Those who will then mount upon the throne and reign. That's the custom over there, again.

His search thus far had failed to yield any of the king's pellets. He'd sidestepped the mission for a brief moment, and now the whole plan has been derailed, so it seemed to them. Water, that's the element in which lies the greatest risk of losing them for good to the smarter. At least, as it pertains to Shadow in these parts of the hood, he doesn't work very well with the water elements of the humanoid world. That much was obvious to him and the girls, and it wasn't good. He wasn't even going to contemplate those possibilities again. Shad will take the blazing, burning fire over water on any given day now, so go. Please bring in the rain to show us how this river flows. No? With fire, there's always a risk of short-term setbacks. But fire doesn't permanently destroy the pellets from the jetpacks. Neither does water, for that matter, nor anything else in the humanoid realms (by the way), on the ideal walk past her, on any given day. But, as for him, water is what he feared the most when it comes to the prospect of him losing the pellets as well as his scanners forever, down the coast, to swim. Or down the drain; by whatever other name, it remains a puff of flames. Fire may burn off and consume the elements that housed the Genodes at any given point in time. But the Genodes themselves will remain intact until they can be recovered from other hosts, acting the part of the house (keeper) or at some other time, no doubt (Mr. speaker). No matter how long it may take him to get out of prison and back to the task of searching them out. Water, though, tends to slow them down and stagnate things a lot, as it relates to the pellets from the kingdom pot. But not the one that he's got now, no, he won't let it part with him and go. A little water will do, and is very much desired in sustaining them, too. But if one should throw them into deep waters, such as in the flood rains, in a river with you. In a lake, a reservoir, or worst of all, in the ocean's depths. Throw them in for an extended period, and those Genodes just seemed to go to sleep, which would be illegal. Shad will take the fire thing over water on any given day now. So, bring it on anyway, anyhow, go. If a fire should burn off the host materials and the surrounding area matter, which housed the pellets. Burn it down to ashes to go and sell it. It will then become a painstaking task to go about sifting through the ashes to find and retrieve the precious pellets, but it can be done. Or one might choose to wait for it to work itself all out. Wait until nature does the job for you to find them, no doubt, and get you gone.

Shadow would have placed the scanners in the needle-pen for safekeeping while being holed up there in the prison camp, and he did, and kept it that way for all of those decades turning into centuries. He kept it carefully hidden from all of these interactions. He dug a hole in the waist-high depth of the mushy leaves that covered the ground like a blanket around them. Before hitting on potter's clay good enough to soak and sound them, like this way "Blow!" He then placed the contents there just below the surface of the clay. Then cover it over with a flat rock right away. Before pulling back the mostly rotten leaves from the bottom up. He then added a layer of freshly fallen leaves on top of it to fill it out. It had by then occurred to him that there was some sort of built-in feature. Some strange mechanism seemed to be on the scanners for the keeper. Or maybe it was a banner for the roaming preacher, I can't quite seem to remember how to reach her with whatever else that might have been needed to hold and keep her, but it was there. That much was for sure, I swear. "Or was it... Wasn't it in the container they were in?" "Of that, he wasn't quite sure to be certain." But it was somewhere around there, near the curtain, he knew it. Or in some other way, it seemed to him to be, in some way, attached even to him, as he was hoping to discover more on this later on as he went along each day (to the inn). But of this much, he was sure. There was something about those pellet scanners. Something was keeping them hidden from everyone else but him, and her, too, yes, his mama, perhaps. Even when in plain view of the rest of them, and you? "No, Pops." They were all the while hidden from anyone else, it would have seemed; from everyone but himself and his team. He'd made an intelligent guess about that, somewhere, and somehow, he thought. Someone else would have those powers, too. The power to make them bow to you, no?

"Maybe." "Maybe those daughters of the king?" He mused about this from within.

The hole that Shadow had dug was as deep as a grave in the mounds of fallen and mostly rotten leaves on the ground, along with the bugs. In those days, you see, the earthworms had not yet immigrated us—ward, nor had they been brought to those parts of the humanoid world for me. So, whenever the trees shed their old, used-up leaves? It would just keep piling up on the forest floor until someone or something came over and stopped it with a sneeze. That something could be fire, a forest fire, as was often the case in those pockets of the brier. At other times or in some other places. It was the people themselves who would have cleared an area out of the forest to build a home along the tracks for the races. A community, sometimes an entire village. In which case, the fire would have been raging and massive. But all in somewhat controlled settings since they must continue to live with the horses, as you'd guessed that such things were, and they are, as is. There were also certain birds and other wilder species that affected these. Some species of reptiles, insects, and bugs, too; other such things were in those times and regional mews. "True". Wilder creatures, which seemed to us to delight themselves in building their nests or otherwise crudely crafted homes out of those fallen and dried leaves. Forest fire, though, was the chief consumer of these dried leaves, no? "No." Yes, the whole forest bore the brunt of those burnings, too, I guess, since the fire did not discriminate as much as you, red dress. "Oh, please!" Sure, not as much as it's known to have happened just as often over there with your earnings fees. That, though, was the good part of the whole thing, as far as it applies to him. The Shadow Man and his mission. He'd also noticed that whenever those burned-out forests came back, spouting triumphant new growths, in fact. All the Genodes from old and burned-out species from the past would also come back multiplied a thousand-fold.

Chapter 8: Random Walk-pass

Once upon one of those times, like this, while some of those humanoid creatures were out again and walking by him, with prop sticks. Something spectacular would have happened that ended up changing the very course of nature for him and me, and Shad would have had a lot to do with it, you see. But, no, don't ask me, I don't know. He was sitting there on the square, though, moping and angry. Sitting there as usual, under his shady tree in the courtyard, held up and humbled by the little school gal... yes, my girl, and getting angrier and angrier by the day. Yes, because he would much rather be out there in the wide-open world, or even in the wilderness, thinking of his girl. If need be, but yes, searching, preferably. Searching and trying to recover his pellets would be the first thing for me. Perhaps it was that. But yes, he was angry at himself for having fallen into such a predicament when so much was riding on him to the regiment, really upset he was. But he was also angry at the captain who had made him an offer with his love, "Let's make a deal," he'd said, divide of the usual laughter on this side of his head. Surely, he had gotten the shadow man's attention and got him to turn his head towards you—"And me?" No mention. "Maybe," he said, "Just maybe you're finding it a little bit hard to sleep around here, with all that noise going on constantly. 'Why bother me?' All of the comings and goings of these strange beings throughout the years, with so many eyes constantly watching you as you try to sleep, you can't sleep in all of that, right? Unlike you, though, I, as well as all of the other guards whom you might happen to see around this place from time to time out here on these dusty belts, and constantly giving you the security eyeing. We do need a little bit of shut-eye now and then. So, here's the deal: I'll let you have that private room over there every once in a while, so that you may get some sleep or even feel for something sweet, my child. You can have it whenever you like, even for a whole week starting tonight. It's all yours, even now, go on, go on. Take it." Sleep? Shadow gulped hard at the very thought of it. He was about to have a fit.

"This is a strange one," the captain said to himself. "He hasn't slept a wink in the last one hundred and thirty years since he's been here on these belts." That, though, was just his estimated guess on the time aspect of Shadow's chronic insomnia since he, the captain, not I, had only been there half that long. But there was a trail of other captains before him, not just one, so he could have been wrong, couldn't he? The astute and very observant captain, though, had noticed the patterns in the registry to show, as well as other tell-tale signs by way of reports from the record books and other officers, guards, and crooks for him to see, you know. They all seemed to suggest that, unlike how it was with those of his own sworn loyal servants, no, not me, but them. Those who had themselves fallen asleep on the job for a time or two, by all accounts and indications, my friends, see them through. This person, their ward and charge, this Shadow Man, now at large and getting a lot worse than worsened, under his hands. He seemed to us to always be awake, alert, and alive. Ever-ready to fight and poised to pounce on the guys.

"Oh, sheet! The fire pit, look at it." Shadow would have discovered this, by chance, that time around. It happened on a day when he was out walking the grounds again by himself. Like he was allowed to do from time to time: Walk around the grounds to keep his mind and body fit and alert for the long haul behind, and to get him back home, perhaps. Yeah! Perhaps it was for that reason. But whatever the cause, he was out there walking again when he'd happened to pounce upon it, the fire pit, and would have happened to scoop up a handful of ashes out of one of the hunter's cold old fireplaces. He discovered a trace of the King's Genodes there for him to go on in and process these, or what seemed to him at the time to be such, like Genode pellets, on the seats, that's what. They were right there amongst the microscopic particles mixed in with the ashes and the soot. But, look, it's now there near his sniffing nose, yes, that part. But hush up and listen, Rose, listen up and be smart. "Uh," the Shadow man grunted. "What have we got here?" He inquired about this further from you and me — a grown kid, bribing us with beers, while the hunter hunted. Well, as I was to hear. "I shall see."

So said he. Stooping down on one knee, he reached in rather gingerly. Yes, with a suspiciously hesitant right hand to feel it out and see. After picking up a pinch of cold ashes, he rubbed it to film on the outer surfaces of his finger and thumb while turning his head this way and then that, Sis. Trying to assure the nightly watches, perhaps that was his reason for the evening's act, Sis, turning his head slowly to glance over each shoulder, covering his back. To reassure himself that he was still alone, again we say, perhaps, since we can't say for sure what this was all about, down home, on the rocks. But he's still got what he's got, that's for sure. And then again. Out of the side bag hanging there across his shoulder. He pulled out the container with the pellet scanners, then dropped one into the ash mat on the ground and started counting on the little boulder. (Since he could no longer count on the chief, Medicine-Shoulder, who was a lot older). His initial air of excitement slowly faded and dissipated into disappointment and frustration when he happened to realize that those pellets he'd found? Although they were, in fact, Genodes from the ground. They were not the genuine Kings' Genodes kind as they're known, for the most part. Nor were there many of those kinds found amongst them, just one. Boy! Did that not hurt the heart? "Yes." Not only did the Genodes get passed on from one form of a host to another, but it was made manifestly clear to him there that day on the border. They'd also multiplied and transformed tremendously on your brother. There were now more copies of the Genodes than were at the start, you see, much more. But only the original King's Genodes kind can be used to do the job back home in those parts; behind those closed Cekko kingdom doors, of sorts. That's where and what. There was a problem, but Shadow was still locked up behind the gate without the key and knew that he didn't have the luxury of a long wait for the come into the office of you and me. The sooner he gets the job done and is on his way home, the better it will be for him and everyone concerned, and he would have saved the day for none more so than for the king and his son, Bauctnumboulei, number one.

Chapter 9: Hunter and the Hunted

Hunter was out again walking. He was seen walking along a trail that he'd hoped would lead him to find as great a game as he had found the last time when he was out hunting. But it had better be quick because supplies were running low back at the camp, and he knew it. Hunter lingered a little too long on the home front before going out on the hunt again, Gord, to go do it. Maybe it was because the last hunt had been so good to him, and he was like, hoping. He wished and hoped that he would be as lucky this time around, too. As lucky as he was then to find a quick kill, like you, and be back home again to give it to whom? "You, I guess." "No, Idris." No need to go rediscovering, reinventing, or remaking the kill, he thought. He would go right back to the same place that was so very good to him the last time he was out. Yes, out there, and hunting. He hoped it would be just as good for him this time, too, old man Bunting. It was good, alright, but it would have taken a bit longer than he'd hoped for. It took him all of those many nights, over four. Hunter was now hot on the trail of the beast. It was of the desired size, he knew it, and gender, too. As the depth of the hoof marks on the trail was able to tell, and as the smell in the moist air was to suggest to you. But the beast was more elusive than any he had tracked before. He was getting hungrier by the end of each day's bidding store. "What is the situation back in the village?" He wondered. He already knew that the supplies back there were running low; he would have known that even before he'd left home to go. The only other person there who was anywhere near ready to go out on a hunt of any sort was his hunter woman of the year. In terms of her being capable, smart, and trained over there. She was the only one who would have been ready and able in that regard. But she was in a state of almost ready-to-deliver something nearer to the navel and the yard; a newborn. He, therefore, must get this kill done soon and be gone, like, to get back to the camp with food. Like, really quick to be good. Like, from yesterday, for that matter, it was that urgent a kick for the round young daughter. His heart cries for help must have fallen onto the ears of the gods, it would have seemed, because he caught up with the beast not many days later, and it was clean. Yes, it was a clean kill. But he was really hungry by then, too hungry to take the trip back to camp on just berries, to take meat back home to them, and cherries. So, he dragged the dead beast under a cave and made a fire. After clearing the surrounding area to prevent the flames from spreading out of control, and going awry. He then hacked away at the strains of his persistent and lingering hunger. As you might have already supposed, and began to wonder. He also hacked into the carcass of the wildebeest and poked around the sleeve as if he was in search of something special, "Oh please!" "Yes." He must have found what it was that he was searching for, because he then cut away with his primitive tools until at last, he came up with delicious, blood-dripping flesh on which he nibbled away while humping out pleasurable groaning and howling with us as if to pray. Sending in his Thanksgiving through every bloody bite there that day. He then struck up a grill over the fire he'd made and placed a wad of flesh on a pole over the flames and smoke he'd raised. Mostly the smoke, blue and white, it spoke. He then feasts on mouthfuls of the (not very well-roasted) flesh. Bite after bite as it became available on his plate. Done up to cave-man perfection, maybe. Or as much as might have been digestible for the thoughts and minds of the humanoid kinds in the KDs, those babies. But as for the hunter... Hmm, hmm, hmm, yeah, he was to become a grunter. He sat and feasted on one bite after another, gluttonous bite, before putting the meaty stick back over the fire to singe and smoke out the other side of it that night, and then taking yet other bites. Shadow, who had been a silent spectator to the sideshow-of-a-savage-feast, up until a moment such as this, now gets the brilliant idea of risking his pellets and scanners by sending them out in the care of his newfound hunter friend to his mama. Since he couldn't taste the meat, maybe, and hoping to find them again. Along with the others, along with the other good ones. He was hoping he'd find them again sometime in the future, the not-too-distant future, preferably. His brilliant idea was to insert the king's Genode pellet, or more like one of the scanners, that's the right way to tell it, Grandma. He inserted it into the body of the (now-stuffed-full and sleeping) hunter. To get him to take it out into the wider universe for him. "And her?" "Maybe." But for sure, to have him take it out into the humanoid world was the idea and more. This was to come about because it was beginning to become clearer to him that he may not make it out of the "holed up" state in which he'd happened to find himself at the time. He reached into the bag for the needle-pen containing the Genode pellets and scanners. He then proceeded to insert one into the sleeping hunter by way of the meaty mound on his backside, handed down to him by his mama. The hunter was jolted back to life and became wide awake upon the impact. Twisting his upper body and shoulders in the process, and spinning around like that. "Like what?"

"Like that. Look at it; the dog. Can't you see the drowsy Labrador searching for its bedhead once more, in the yard?" "Oh Lord! Is it scarred?" "Yeah! Look at that." Now, discard. Hunter slapped one heavy hand onto the spot and rubbed violently at it while fanning away at an imaginary insect, I think. Then did it again with the other hand, you bet, now sweat, and wink. He was fanning at an insect on whom the hunter himself had placed the blame for stinging him while he slept near the fire in the camp, properly. For surety, Shadow also inserted one of the pellet scanners, to be precise, my brother. He inserted it into the dead carcass of the wild beast. There, look, right there, where it was dirty. Nearer to the ear than the eye of the feast. The hunter probably did not want to risk further attacks from the violent, wilder creatures in the place. So he put out what remained of his fire and picked up his kill over his broad, strong shoulder, then headed home, back to base, towards the cowards in the yard near the big boulder, his homely space. This is how it happened there at the time, as I was to hear it coming from the lying... Whilst the hunter slept in his camp, brought on by the effects of the overeating operation, the cramps. Yeah! Ate until he was cramped, you know. Shadow waltzed right in and administered his numbing agents. This was also tweaked to ensure that the subject continued to sleep throughout the operation on the pavement, and he did. Shad then got to work grafting the finest and most attractive carvings the humanoid eyes had ever seen. Such carvings were grafted onto the skin of the slumbering hunter while he was slumbering away in his dreams. Far away from the dumpster and his many queens, but then again. He also had to place them in places on the body that could not be concealed from view. It must always be seen by all of them and you. "Aah, aah, aah," yeah! Just like you, he was aahing away at the waking dew. Yes, sir, he was to become an Aah-er too. After seeing them, the hunter never knew, no. He never knew what had hit him, and you. But nothing has been the same since then, who knew! When he got back to the village, dragging home his kill. The carcass of the wilder beast, if you will, dragging it home for them to feast on. As always before, the youngster would have been the first out of the dumpster to meet and help him haul the prize over the final few steps through the door, and home, Sir. And sure enough, they did. But the youngsters were more excited this time than ever before at the gig. Hunter was bringing home something more than usual this time for them and the kids. Much more than the corpse of the dead boar from somewhere around the pigs. As was the norm for them to storm him over there on those wilderness shores of his, and as may be seen happening now in his homeland territories. Look, look at it through this little thing. Can you see it? Yes, their eyes were more focused on the body of the hunter than the beast he was dragging home for dinner; many dinners in feasts for many moons to come, like these, now happening back home, on the inner... even. Apart from the carcass of the wild beast. The hunter was seen dragging home some strange markings on his own body for their eyes to feast on. The inhabitants of the primitive village could not keep their eyes off them. They were the most beautiful things that they had ever seen in their entire lives, amen, according to ever-after events and the songs that were to be heard singing off into the nights, by them. Although Hunter had been warning them of how painful it was for him, he'd also noticed that, over time, the pain did seem to subside somewhat. It didn't take long for the whole village to take notice of the dumb nut.

"Of-of, of what?" What dumb... something.

Yeah, man! That too, and him, and you, and then everybody wanted one. "I want one of those things" was going to become the latest tune in town. Very quickly, too, it became number one. "True." Shadow was keen to be mean when he left a container of his mixture in plain view of the hunter. Along with a copy of his tattooed needle pen, a special gift to them from the grunter, it was meant, Sir. You know, meant to be, and just like he'd scripted it in his mind, the hunter took both of them straight home, along with the things from behind. Yes, his hindquarters, the beast's carcass, and the bones. So started the Age of the Tattooed, starting first from right there within the village camp and his home. Then spread outward to you, and me, and them, and then, as more time went by. People began to look in on them and spy. Then they went to immigrate even further into many and varied parts of the universe, but don't ask me why. Please, I'm getting a bit tired of these. Yeah! I know, you are too. But, go on, go ahead and sue.

The tattoo culture and hence, the Genodes and Scanners were likewise finding their way across many waters, infiltrating the lifestyles and customs of many peoples around the globe. Over the next several thousand years, the tattoo arts migrated and spread across many regions and took on deep roots in such places and cultures as Samoan culture, Polynesian, Maori Tribes, and New Zealand. Buddhist culture. China, Japan, the United States of America, India, Thailand, Ireland, Egypt, Mexico, and many more such places and cultures to go. Thanks to Google and Wikipedia for these statistics. We've got to be sure to satisfy you and the rest of the critics. The age of the Tattoo has now been firmly established, carrying along with it the King's Genodes in the goblets, he'd hoped, and the scanners, no joke. Half the work is now done for the Shadow man, as he was to be seeing things at the time, from the top of the pan: It now remains only for him to go out searching and finding; he needs to go search for and find them, if he can, anyway he can. He must go find those original Genodes, or at least half of them, plus the BEACON. Yes, that one, and get them back home by the weekend, and back to the Kingdom and the king, whose son was still in a static state and risks remaining that way into all eternity, if the only thing that could change that situation doesn't show up quickly.

Chapter 10: Get Him Out of That Prison

Is it a bird, or a reptile, a pterosaur, perhaps? "I was there looking at things coming in and wondering when..."

Yes, that's him there, talking. Shad was sitting there in the courtyard again, sitting on the smooth rock, yay, on that fateful day, scratching. His back up against the trunk of a tree, needless to say, watching them, as usual. That was when he saw it; he caught a glimpse of something. "Look!" he whispered from his gut within. There are tiny dark spots out there on the horizon, approaching and becoming larger on the moves to come in and bite beside them and him, encroaching. Unmoved he was, other than for a turn of the head to look this way and then that.

"At the bugs, right?"

"No, not that, but..." He was looking around, trying to ascertain whether anyone else might have seen it. Not yet, it would have seemed, but they sure will soon. He knew that much before noon. Here they come, there are many, much more than one, as it would seem to any, and then. Listen now to him, the captain, and the others with him; he's talking to the rest of them. Or is he?

"What is this?" He asked rhetorically. The captain had finally zeroed in on the action and was fixing to engage the visitors, but on his terms to a last-minute fraction, wanted to score a retreat with her, you know. He didn't bargain on what was about to hit him square in the face next, though. "Deh suh?"

"Yes, there, sir. Besides the sunburns, the lower fifth-quarter row, and the bushy hair. Look at it, right there, it's rolling now on the recorded spheres." The captain is taking notice; he's looking up now, up towards the open skies. "Mi blow-wow, awah dis?" asked someone who looks a lot like a Jamaican, look at his... One by one, the others are joining in, shading their eyes even. They're shading it from the glare of the noonday sun hanging over them. The heart of it seemed to be now just above the approaching things or people. As was to be seen from his standpoint and where he is now, pointing at it, and the vehicles. But the army is coming in, still, or whatever that thing is, it is still coming. Chill! Now, every living soul in and around the camp is caught up in the mystery and the magic of the moment, that's what. "What is what is what this is this is this?" They were all chiming in one after the other, spewing the spits at the brother. All (seemingly) forgot that they were soldiers and guards. rather than spectators, starry-eyed spectators to an overhead show as seen coming into the yards, and in for another spectacle of sorts. But no, it wasn't a passing stage show. By the time they would have managed to catch up with their fleeing senses and wits, and started reaching to take hold of their weapons to go do it. It was way too late for them. A late show for all of them there behind the gated stare through it, and that was when... Zoo-oosh zoo-oosh-oosh, tooosh, the fireballs were zooming in to do it. Streaming in upon long trails of smoke, behind the head and of the strings like spokes on the cords, and digging in to do it. You know, to do its work and go. Digging into the ground, like so, and into some backsides brown too, you bet. "No!" "Yes." Even into the inner skin of some of them, after they would have blasted through the flesh and bones of scared-out-of-their-wits and scampering away soldiers, guards, and the Shadow man alike. Everyone in the yard was running away like mice. But this might have been nothing more than a practice run for the girls of the day; some sort of foreplay for their crew, I'd say. "Or was it, wasn't it, a scare tactic of sorts for them to do?"

"Oh, maybe it was something else like you, so go." Some other things, such as that tick on the horseshoe, no? Could have been, you know. Because, after they'd zoomed in and caught up with him, yeah, the Shadow man. They grabbed a heavy-handed hold of him, on the run, and were screaming, while laughing as if they were glad for the fun, and beaming. They lifted him onto the right riding side of the beast, yes, on the backside of the Zebra-striped beastly meat. Then they turned around and just as quickly as they had come in, they were going out again. Gone riding away with the Shadow man as a pillion rider behind one of them. An unwilling but tired pillion rider he was, on the right riding side of one of those said Zebra-striped beasts of the girls. He was sitting behind the second in line of those fighting girls. "That one would have been Noella, right?" Of course, she was. Shad knew them very well; he'd seen them many times before in his life and times as his friends, but never in action. Or at least, not this kind. Not this type of action, no, not like this. He sure as hell wasn't counting on ever being favored with such pleasures again. No matter on which end of their peace and passivity he might happen to be found fallen. But yuck, tough luck; from here, the road leads home to Cekkoland on the square. It might have been based on the fact of not sleeping for all that time. Or was it just from being in the comfort of familiar friends and the fine ones? Well, whatever the reason, it wasn't long after the hoist up onto the backside of the beast that Shadow was to be found there fast asleep. Good for them, good for the girls on the ride in, because they were concerned about how he would have taken to them and their methods to get him out of prison. But so far, it's a good ride in. It's all good to go, on the way home to Cekkoland on the stone at the ninth end, no? "Yes, you know!" "What?"

It's been a long time since Shad has been back home, but as of yet, he hasn't seen anyone. Well, not the people he would like to see and to have a little chat with over tea and fried green onions. As of yet, he hasn't seen the king, nor any of the friendly folks known to him. Other than for Smokey, the last person he wanted to see. No joke, Leigh, really. Not after what he had done to him, and you, and me, to get him out on a search and rescue mission properly. But, just as always with him, the Shadow man? Tough luck, yes, that one. He's stuck with Smokey, who is now hacking at him and getting him carved out and stuffed (Turkey). But then, one day, it was to get home to him that this wasn't the end. He was going back out on the road again. To go and finish off the task that he had gotten started on, for them, and to bring the pellets home on the star grid, home end. It was just a pit stop for refueling and some bodily checkups, too, just a shoo-in. As soon as the job was done, he was going back out with the scouts. No joke. That's how it went. Smokey got to work chipping away at the many baked-on "vice," those that the Shadow man would have picked up in the fields and on-site. Like, like the thing that had kept him in jail for so long, that's right. It was a spell that they'd cast on him to render him invisible to humanoid beings. But it was nothing that Smokey wasn't able to handle... him. Smokey had for himself a hard task working all night on that massive piece of glass. But he was good enough and would have managed to chisel him out of the rough. And then, it was show time again, time for the Shadow man to be sent back out on the road with them. That was when the girls were sent for again. Which, surprisingly to them, wasn't to pose a problem. Shad was willing and ready to go back out there with them. His only hope was to see his friend, Liam. But that was not part of the plan, no, not one, no, not one, now, move along and away from that song; it's not a good plan at this time. Old habits tend to die hard, because as was to be seen from behind her hands, holding the saddle cord. Smokey knows only one way to get agents out of the yard. Or two; one for the girls, the other for him, and you, or anybody else who (for any reason) may need to go out with kingdom things to do. They must be loaded up with Smokey's secret sauce. So, the girls were called back into the class and made ready to go fast. For the ride back out with Shadow Needleman, the unconscious load was unsteady, little one. The cargo is now heavily laden on the car to go back out on the second leg of his mission. No, this type is not for poppy shows; fire up the ignition. They then took the long ride out of camp, out of the territory, and off to another faraway place at once, with me. Way out of the reach of those jailors ever having any chance of getting their claws again onto the most valued Cekko kingdom agent of theirs, with any intent to hinder him or do him wrong by way of harming his ears. They then dropped him off in the depths of the distant wilderness. Somewhere over there, far away from here, yes. On another continent, even so, I was to hear. With a charge for him to get on with the job, the real job of finding and returning the lost Genodes home to Bob. And then, just as quickly as they came, they were gone, going out again. But as for him, the Shadow Man?

Like an eagle, look, there he was. sitting on the leafy mat carpet of the forest floor amongst the bugs. His back was resting against the trunk of a huge tree again. Just a short measure from where he'd fallen when the girls had dropped him off there and then, that was many years earlier. He was free to go wherever he wanted to and do whatever he may, but he was still there, across from you. Just sitting there and fanning away at the wilder bugs that were hell-bent, I hear, oh! Wait a minute, was it hell that they were bent and sent from? Or somewhere else within it? Damn, I don't really know, man. But, but... Anyway, be it hell, or wherever else it might have been that they were from, or were supposed to go and tell. They were nonetheless there, bent on skinning him alive. Mincing him up to swallow, against his will, to survive. He fanned away at them and grunted; it was as if he did not know that he was free. But you didn't hear it from me, kid, okay? "Oh! Poor thing, look at him." It was more or less like this, as it was to be seen happening there in practice. Like an eagle hatched and raised by chickens from the rats' nest, then when the chicken coop's door was flung open, the open skies beckoned to him. The eagle would not take flight up to the skies because... Go ask him if you think I'm lying... down. In his mind, he was a chicken, still. So, although the Shadow man was snatched up by the fighting girls and crew when they happened to pass by the jail where he had been held up with them and you for all that time. They'd happened to pass by and snatched him away. They then headed home to Cekkoland with him for a shower and a remake, and then brought him back and deposited him out there on the open wilderness floor on display, a mistake. Shadow, for his part, though, was still in a prison state, it seemed. In his mind and his heart, row. "You, you mean?" "Yes." So he sat there for years. Just sitting there for a very long time. Fanning away at them, yes, mankind, and getting fat with those bugs, his friends, but then. After a while, he started to wander out and out and then further out from there, in style. Yes, out from the point where he'd fallen. Over time, he'd finally discovered that he was styled-up and "well-loved" by his darling. Because he was able to act on his own account, do things, and control the outcomes of them, the hosts had finally come calling on him. Well, so it would have seemed to me, and them. It was then that the old Shadow man began to realize that he was indeed free. Many decades would have elapsed by then, though, centuries probably. But Shadow Needleman didn't become the great and trusted agent he had by then managed to have become by just a whim. He really earned his stripes from them. Some of them were grudgingly giving it over to him, after all the fuss from among them, and arguing. He knew right there and then that he had to get moving on and away from those joints. He needed to get back to the task at hand and back to the job of that, not brewing beer pints. No, not that, but the real job. The "real" job, as you already know, was to go out and get the Genodes from wherever in the world they might happen to be at the time, and get them as well as himself home. Getting the job done and getting a move on home and off the road; it was his only real kingdom task to complete and upload. It had not been easy getting that "far," for the lack of a better term, at parr, so... Shad knew that it would not be easy moving on from there either. From where he was at the time and on the meager. But moving he must. "Oh!" he said to himself after he had come back to his senses, which he would have reached up and taken back down off the shelf, to rest them firmly upon the benches. Well, perhaps. But it felt to him as if it were something out of a movie in a picture, or something. More or less like those smiley thing fixtures with cornmeal dumplings. Those things that the humanoid kind have been immersing themselves in of late, and in the store's sink too, my sisters, while wiping the slate. Or, it was more like, like an old soul, it seemed, might have died tragically, long ago, probably, and is now reborn in his body, and wanted to get on with the job, and to go tell it to somebody, like, his story, and much more of the gory, as it is when wrapped up in the details. So it would have seemed to him and me, and you too in those days, I'm sure. "I've got to get back to some unfinished business," he said to himself through the burst of his sneeze. Got things to fix. This was at times conflicting for him, since he couldn't quite tell when he asked this: is a nine and a stick some sort of trick to go out and fix six? But, uh, what's this?

Yes, wordplay is the order of the day around here.

Chapter 11: The Quest

Returning now to the question at hand. Shadow Needleman was given a second chance to complete the task after he was busted out of prison at last, and after he visited with soothe sayers, and had the maggies ministered on his finer things for him and his layered ass... As such, instructions were given by the boss and the king. After all, he was, at the time, still their best agent. The very best person for the job is about to call all of the pearly lots back into the regiment. So they thought, at the very least, my good gentlemen. But he had to turn his attention back to the original task: the one he was sent out to do at first, since you'd asked. That was to go out, find and return the original Genodes pellets and the scanner's home to the kingdom and the house in Paris. All of them, preferably, or at least seven of them, including the BEACON, for me. "That would have been enough," they said to me, for them to be able to reset and restart the process of the day. But Shadow wanted them all; he was never known as one to settle for less than the very best outcome on any call. No matter what, he was to be found doing at any time as given. Was that what led to his undoing and the fall? Probably. The BEACON, as you already know, is the man. He's the lead one, somewhat like the chief pellet among the Genodes. With it, one may be able to trace, track, and attract other lost or missing Genode back to the place. But without it, one can do almost nothing. Oh, sheet, what's this, a dumpling in this plate? "No, it's..." Unless such a one should have all of the other twelve Genodes altogether in one place. This is not the case now, as you can see from the writings on his face, wow! And then, such a one must also know the code as to how to arrange and manipulate those twelve Genodes to draw in the thirteenth, the BEACON.

Or to spot its signals from wherever in the universe that it may be at the time, asking for the weak one, I mean, Lee Gwan, the blind general, and his queen. Then, such a person must also know how to get it into their pockets and get it home to them. So he will need to go out into the far reaches of the universe, searching, to try and find at least six of the other Genodes to go along with the BEACON on his purse string before he can return home. "Home?" "Yes, have you ever heard of such a place?" "Oh boy!" He was almost ready to cry on his face, no joy. He started a new search where he'd already have a leg up. Shad's first quest from that place was to visit the North Pole and stand there from sunrise to sunset, which could last up to six months in humanoid time measures, as you had guessed. Depending on what season of the year it may be when one gets there, yes. He could even be there a whole year if he's not very careful, I guess, dear. But then again, Shadow Needleman was not planning on leaving things up to mere chance, Sis. He was still busy on some other fronts, doing cross-species dances, grazing on bunny bumps, even. While still out there, scanning through undocumented nuances and breeding among heathens. But now, he must move on to other regions where the Genodes might be circulating, just waiting to be retrieved by someone like him. But then came the entrance of those girls, again. The girls of the earthling kind would have ridden in and all over him, my friends, and upset the apple cart some more before he could get the job done for them, and be gone for sure. Or more like, they were the ones preventing him from getting the job done, by giving him a whirlwind of a whacking down in the earthlings' hometown.

"Am I the living, or the dead?" He was heard asking this from the open in his head. "Who is it that has returned in me?" he asked. But then again, he still knew enough to know that there was yet more work to be done and that he had to get a move on, fast. To accomplish the task that was still very much at hand. So, he started from there, slowly. Just following a path as it was laid out in front of him, my dear Udahlee. Where? There. Look and listen on. "Have you ever seen anything like this before?" he wondered out loud from behind the bore. On the backside of speaking out loud, you know. Yes, the flip-flopping door, that one even, and more. It was like... like someone had carved a path out of the landscape and laid it on the wilderness floor. "Straight." According to the way my countrymen would have said it back home at the High Gate. So, the Shadow Man followed that path and walked on in the direction it led him through the park. From there onward, if you'd asked. Yes, that part, homeward, as he'd thought. This was to be the entrance into more humanoid worldly mess and into yet more trouble than he'd bargained for, as you might have guessed, so, look. He's out of the wilderness now and walking, yes, Mass Vin, walking on the road that is about to lead him into a myriad of other troubles. Some, from which he will not recover. At least not without another trip back to base. Back home for a refresher course, some refueling, and a Cekko shower too, to chase. Such as might be more than needed in this case of iced tea, and at the final hour for him and you, not me.

...

Picture this: A dark wilderness with a column of smoke billowing upward into the skies. Imagine you're standing afar off and looking out over this mountain range on the heights. You can surely see the mountain range. The smoky column, too, is rising over the range and pointing to the skies, true. But you can't tell from where you're standing what may be going on there among the trees and on the wilderness floor. Now, picture this, too, a little bit more, coming at you from a different point of view than before. Toady, the toad, is hopping around on the wilderness floor, spying in. He's there on a mission, eyeing him. He's out on a mission to track and keep a watchful eye on the activities of the agents who might be there at any time, as given. Toady was sent out there to disrupt and manipulate whatever the agents may be seeing of the goings-on with the pellets, and what they might be doing at any given time. He was also told to report back to the chief agent and the ranger at the palace near the base of the shrines. Those glistening marble pillars tend to leave someone like me and you blind. Picture further: Picture Shadow, the super-agent sent down below. He's now there on that same wilderness floor; he doesn't know about the toady agent yet, I'm sure. But Toady knows him, everything about him, and a whole lot more. Now, the toad is programmed to favor night travel over all else. For him to avoid certain things, and like, overall hell. Toady was commissioned to avoid the lights of the day. Working under the cover of the night, one might say. But then again, that was the very thing that was going to lead him headlong into other things and people. The Shadow Man even. Toady knew how to hop around town, it would have seemed, like how to hide and run on Steam. Even racehorses know how to do that and do it well, I mean, what the hell! Where's the fun I'm in? Come on in, hop into the van! I'm leaving.

Yes, wordplay is the order of the day around here. Yeah, man, a Jamaica yaad mi come from, sorry, I meant to say, I'm Jamaican born and bred, okay?

Chapter 12: After the Pain of Those Women

All alone now, he's walking. Shad is out and walking along a road that often disappears and reappears from where we are. But not very far from our standpoint in the car, a little bit removed from the coastline sometimes. Look nuh, mi star. Sulking along the sometimes-boisterous waves of the river, the road continues, hastening on to go and deliver. Winding away along the other side of town were inlets, hamlets, and bays, too, which added the extra day, laughter, and even the flair into its journey ever after; this is where it was. Along the shore, on the glad journey down to the harbor, once more, and there in the yard. Oh lord! Look. There's a colorful maple tree or two, here and there. Depending on the access in view, and on what season of the year. There are ornamental decorations there to stop the staring eyes and to break up the peer through. All are there to keep out the intrusion into the homesteader's privacy. "And you?" I'm keeping some preferred hidden things from view, no inquisitive eyes to see, and like staring somewhere when you're there and hearing those voices from behind the croutons and pine trees asking those who might be passing, "Who are you?" All along, on its silvery flow, the river goes on a roll, rolling, on the way to go off, craving for the lights of the big city of modern-day earthlings' commercial activities, and even further afield. The river rolls on like this, those, and these. She's never satisfied, it would have seemed, she never rests her heel. It was not like Shadow didn't know that the river was there. He's been walking these roads ever since his reluctant arrival here. Of course, Shad would have declined the offer; it was rather generous of them, though, really, no laughter. Shad had declined the bed they'd offered to him, yes. "Or even a place in the straw, sir." Said another of the dress... yes, they'd said such things to him. Whichever one was to be found preferable for him to sleep in, on the cloth, even. No, he wouldn't steal the grit from the other's offered offerings upon a draw to reveal it to them, or the offspring. He wasn't about to be found rolling around in a stinky-smelling, farmyard-like barn either. He would accept neither of the two. The next homey roof to cover his slumber, he had long pledged to himself and her. Would be home-bound, his very own. Whether it is to be one on this side of the distant divide or back there in the place where he rightfully belongs and calls it home. He wasn't planning on staying around these parts for too long a time. Some way, somehow, he knew he would be going back to the faraway place he had long known and called home, but was sure that those of the earthlings' way would not understand the first thing about that, and would not be made to. But what does he know about anything, either? He will soon find out where the road leads her from here. Or will not. Shadow then guided his steps along the pavement that abruptly turned left and then crossed over a narrow bridge, where he would have looked out over the glistening waters towards the brave men and contemplated. To the right of him, the coastline stretched out, gently embracing the silver ripples on the water's edge, no doubt. To the left, look, there it is. Farmlands and sporadic houses, and the other bridge, like the big one, a bit further beyond the small one. Look, can you see them there? Barnes and feeder bins, too. They were still trotting along beside him. "True." "I know, that's why I said so. Ugh!" Just as they are prone to be found doing with me and you, on the ride in. But with nothing to do, seemingly. Nothing other than for feeling me, and you, are you going to...? A scene that was vaguely familiar to him. Yes, it was familiar to some faraway scenes from his boyhood, I'm guessing this. As you already know, I would, little miss. Yes, hiss! Good. Set firmly in the deep recesses of his mind. But yes, it's all good. It was in the forests around those parts where he caught the first glimpse of it that time. His first sighting of Toady the toad, not the swine, but it was the funniest thing for him to acquit and go sign. It was while marooned there under the evergreen trees that he saw it at first and began to contemplate and ponder the sad turns of events that had brought him there in the first place. Of course, he didn't make much of the sightings then, "Just frogs, my friend," he said, with the worst taste, to him. It's just a toad in its element. He was the intruder there; he knew that much. But that was to be only the first of many such sightings of the jumping thing before there was to come the touch, and then... Shad was sitting there in the wilderness, again. Under what was by then becoming his favorite place to just sit and waste time away with friends. He had seen it before he knew it; a time or two, or three. "Goodness gracious me!" so said he. "Look!" Surprised he was to see. There it is again, the toad, my friend. Perched atop the dead log, lying there on the forest floor, along with them. Along with all the other woodland things, and more, my good friend. Unlike how things are in Cekkoland, where, as for the rest of them, there... You know. There are other toads or frog-like creatures over there in those regions, with toes. But as you already know how these things are prone to going down there on the lonely roads. One is likely to hear them long before seeing them. But no, not this one, not so with him. This toad was just sitting there looking at him, looking back at him. And then, out of the blue, it would have happened to you. "No." Yes. He would have spoken to you and him, even in proper Cekko language, my friend. "When are you going to get it done and over with?" The creepy, jumpy thing said in the talk to him while spewing out the spit, at his head's fast spin, you know, around it, oh sheet! Look out! Had to duck out of the way, you know, and fast, to save his bed when he gets back home, at last. Shad did not respond, not in words at the time, just turned and stared at it from there. Looking at him still there and talking, scared. In the meantime, Shad was standing there and scratching his head with his shaky hand, and staring at the homely bed through the distant lens, yes, yet more. "Have you found any of them yet? You can't be sitting around wasting time when there's work to be done." "Who are you? Who sent you here?" Shad could be heard asking him when he'd found his tongue again, my dear… offspring. Yes, though it was still in there, somewhere, go ask him. But somehow, he couldn't seem to find it before. But that was precisely the moment when Toady chose to skip the scene. To be gone quickly out the door, I mean, and away from him. Leaving him there to blink at the rapids and wonder about what he'd just seen. "What's going on with me?" wondered the Shadow man, and cap-scratching his lean… something, still. That wasn't the first time Shad had seen that toad; he was sure of it. It was not going to be the last time either, mi blood. (Turned and spit). Never before had he found the need to use the special inputs from his journey kit. But he sure has a reason to use them now, to furnish a fix. He reached into the side bag and fished out the trinket box. He then went to work assembling the rod and whipped up the magic potion flux. Wherever the Shadow man went thereafter, his ever-ready, in-service rod was close at hand, good master. It wasn't very long after that, when he was to run headlong into his opportunity in the form of Toady the toad, again. Or it could have been more a case of him being more alert and on the lookout for the same wild creature. "That thing?" Yes, that might have been why he was so quick in spotting it the next time around the bend, and waiting to greet her with chimes and drums, my friends. Whatever the case, though, there it was. No, not on the go, but on the forest floor at that time. Mixing and mingling with the tree droppings, the weeds on the ground, the bugs, and the grime. Trying, it would seem, to conceal itself from the Shadow man's view. In its dreams, maybe! But it was not to be this time, because things are different lately, and at last, look. He would have been quick to see it; he saw it there. He already had the rod in his hand. Having the potion in a container in the side bag close at hand, Shad reached into the bag, fished out the potion, and flashed a couple of sprinkles in the toad's direction. In the direction of where the toad was, you know, yes, it was there, boss man. "Yuh mean, 'Deh suh?'" No, right there, it's better when said that way, you hear, like so. Trying to hide among the dried leaves and weeds, and pretending as if it wasn't, doing these. Too late for that, too late for the hiding part for Toady, not the cat. So now, Shad is talking, in some rather strange languages unknown to you and me in these parts, and parting... He's not talking to the toad as of yet, just talking, you bet. It's probably a part of the routine used to get the magic to work for him. It's working for sure. The toad bows its head and folds up, and as it were, falls asleep on the ground floor. Shad then took hold of the beast and went about performing yet more rituals on the legs of the thing to go feast. Hours later, it woke up, hopped away, and out of there, in haste. He intended to continue working on the task for a few more days, yet, so I hear. You know, whatever the task was that he had started to perform on the toad. It would need to be continued over several days down the road, and even more, like, when carrying the load, in... But then, look. Look at that thing; a bobcat. A Bobcat had been sneaking around now and then and peeping around the bend. Peeping around a tree or two to see what he could do about this mouthful of delightfully un-stewed chew, probably true. That same one is sitting there already, across from you, maybe. Been there all night. It may have been there for some time, long before daylight, mankind. But... what's that? Look, a chipmunk, what is that? Is it drunk? The chipmunk scampered away after coming upon him, somewhat unaware. Then came a deer, oh dear, he looked at it and said, "Hello there!" Yeah, the deer seemed to hear; that's why it ran across the forest floor, right there. Ears standing tall, eyes looking, inquisitive know-it-all. Boys cooking, or something. It was turning around the fall as if searching for something or someone to call. Look, its nose is wrinkling, twitching, and sniffing the air. To catch the scent of whatever or whoever it is that could be there, perhaps. Long ears stood up tall, focused attention zeroing in from every direction. Did he see someone? Did he see him, the Shadow Man, for instance? Or was it just an instinctive response? Like, a built-in mechanism for self-preservation? Probably that one, look at that. She ran, she ran away. And now, look.

Chapter 13: Mounting up on wings

Up, up, look up there over and above his head, there they go floating on by. Mounting upon the wings in midair. "Oh, how I wish that I could still fly." He grunted this within my oh — "Well, if he could, but, no, not mine, not this time. So..."

"Okay, just go, get thee behind..." Because things were always happening around and about him, but much further afield than he could see with the naked eye from within the humanoid inserts of what his eyes had at the time happened to be in disguise. He sat there, just outside the modern-day commercial district of the earthlings, where... Yes, he was just sitting there at this point and wasting time away, the worst thing. Painting the scene by the day, I'd say. One brushstroke at a time of day. The ornate lettering on billboards was screaming out at him, at everyone, as a matter of fact, to spin. It wasn't just him getting fattened up there and skinned. But as for him? He would not react. At least not in ways as the merchants might have thought, but they were there, offering everything to spare. From a pin to an anchor, all their precious wares, and the tares too, like money for the banker, yes, they were, lurking over there and waiting for you. They were offering healing for any and everything that ails him. Yet he ached in places he didn't even know that he had muscles before the tailspin. No one was able to find a cure for it, it would have seemed. No sprouts from Brussels to go along with the beans. Because, as for him, there was no such convenient remedy there for what ails him, really. "It..." that thing that was at the time, nailing him to the pit: The longing, the sudden burst of homesickness, was a sobering witness and a constant reminder to him that he was yet another stranger wandering in a faraway land. Trying hard to stop himself from chasing those things behind her hand. A shop was there for everything; every needed item for him, each desire fulfilled. But as for me? "I don't know how any of it works, man, because it sure doesn't work for me," so lamented Shadow to nobody in particular, Leigh. But still, he was sitting in the shadow of the old-growth tree. Eventually, though, he had to go like so, "blow-wow," that's when he did it. He had to slap himself up and move along, again, with the heavy right hand of his mind, my friend, on a shoestring. Because the hands hanging there by his side were way too heavy to be lifted with the residue of what was left of his strength for the slapping behind... Or maybe they were too feeble at the time. Those arms of thine, Shadow, may have been much too lightweight to have been able to summon up the desired effect. Had they, the limby arms of death, I'd say, had they been the things that had slapped you awake, up and moving on? No, I don't think so, mate. Just grooving along on all eight, go on, go, get the plate, and no, it's not a mistake. You might cross the bay by boat from here, or on a raft, then cross a road and walk a few steps further out there, or in the park. Depending on how one may choose to look at it from there, and then. It was blue out there, bluish-grey, more or less like a pair of cold lips never having been kissed, I'd say. Probably never will be. Surely, not like this — hmmmuah kiss, from me. But he's now there, alone again... no, not with me. And there on the cliff overhanging the bay, one might sit and look across the years, even with longing eyes and weeping tears. Legs hanging low and dangling, oh my. More or less like materials from a ballerina's trinket box on opening night. "At the Ranglin's, right?" "Probably right." One might even look out and out yet further, and out still on the harbor. Until what's left of the sun would subside, tumbling down beyond the fault line right before your very eyes. But then again, maybe some other time, guys.

Slowly, he's walking past the graveyard, wearing his dark skin and as crazy as... But he doesn't know a thing about such things; he doesn't know what it is, nor how these things go. But he's still walking, Syl, and singing a song, to thrill. One of his favorite Marley songs, perhaps. One such as: Wake up and live, yeah, wake up and live. Nervously, he was slowing it down and turning to stare at them at regular intervals, while looking around at them as if at the gal he had never had. He had never seen one like this before, of that, he was sure. He doesn't have such things over there where he came from. There won't be any when he gets back home to the kings' dome either, no matter how long... Such things over there, as you already know, will never be. Done. Shad had spent the night there, resting his tired feet (unscared was he). At first, when he'd sat himself down on the smooth rock. Yeah! That's what he thought it was at the time: a rock. But then, he fell asleep there, just like that; too tired to carry on, another step away from here, to the bus stop. That too was even though he had lost his confidence in the routine over here, and you... The sleeping routine, I mean, you bet, my dear. He can't trust the sleep routine anymore, but yet, here's the score. The silvery moon was shining brightly on the landscape when he opened his eyes and saw the writing on the stone. The upright part of the stone where he wanted to go over and sit, yes, to sit down. At first, it was hard for him to decipher what it was. There were some scribbled markings, that's all it was to him. But it wasn't long afterward that it was made manifestly clear to him what it was. The whole thing, as was to be seen in these writings upon the stones. "Here lies the remains of the late Murphylus Pitters, sunrise..." "Aah!" he exclaimed. "So, that's how it is done in this neck of the woods? The humanoid kind is a species that can expire, or be extinguished, too, to be good. And this is how they handle such events? Who knew?" "You would? Okay." From that point on, he'd purposed it within himself to walk very softly and slowly and to take the time necessary to learn as much as he could about the intricate workings of the humanoid kinds, and their doings. There were many of them there, very many, in one small, well-outlined, and well-manicured area on the square, and compact. Relatively speaking... "About what?" "That, but like, when talking to you and me in this case of iced tea swap." He would have hastened to get away from there as quickly as possible, just as a thought. Not so much out of his fear of them, nor any such thing like that. But more out of a feeling of reverence for them and the folks who might be offended by it. Do you know what I mean? Like, by seeing a stranger loitering there. Or even if it should be sometime in the future, one might be prone to becoming offended by hearing that a strange, wandering outsider had been loitering around their loved one's burial site. Shad didn't want to risk that, right? But alas! The girls would have ridden in and upset the apple cart before he could get the job done, and rode his mount back home astride his horse named Noam. So now Shadow is back in the safety of the Cekko kingdom, again. He's talking to them and the king, telling him things, including this particular part of the story, and all the other events that had happened to him, even. The king is more than a little interested in hearing from the Shadow man. Particularly, this part of the plan, and to hear the rest of the earthly mystery, coming out of his hand, from you and your... not mine, Mitzie.

Reflections. There came a time when another conversation was overheard in a distant realm. It happened between the then forcibly retired and shipped home Shadow Needleman and another, whom we'd supposed was his friend, the great one himself, King Liam. It was in this wise that the conversation came through to us while we were sitting idly by, out there on the bus, must I...? "No." "So, buddy, how was your trip?"

"Hard, much harder than was expected."

"Oh Lord! How so?"

"You know! It gets hard out there at times. It was like, like, different. Like, for instance, you know. Those times when those searches along the way felt as if they were leading me nowhere, or even worse than that curse, like, when it seemed to me as if they were leading in the wrong direction, like, away from here."

"Did it happen that way often? Did it happen a lot like that?"

"A few times over the centuries, as a matter of fact. You know! I thought you were always there looking out for me... for my greatest good. Like you'd said to me when your word was good. Did you not say that you would have been watching over me, or at the very least, that you would be there for me? I thought you would have been there for me, man, like, whenever things and times get rough and tight. Which, by the way, happened a lot." He was quick to say this and that. "...Or at least some of those times, like, when I was locked up in that rotten jail, for instance. You should have been there to help. But you were not, ever. What happened? How come you were never around?"

"I never promised you a rose garden; those flowers are grown. I never promised you I would 'always' be there watching over you, did I?"

"I beg your pardon! What am I—"All I said was that I would be looking out for your greatest good and safe return home, and as you can see for yourself, even now, look, look at it. You're, in fact, home, and safely so, no?" "Oh man... and look at what you made me do. If only I knew that you weren't there hovering over me all the time, I wouldn't have..."

"You wouldn't have what? What did you do over there that I still don't know about?"

"Nothing, nothing at all, man, oh man."

"What now? What did you do? Tell me, or not do for that matter, as it would seem to me like the latter is the case here?"

"Never mind me, my dear King. What was done was over there with them and him. And it's already done, you hear, and it's, it's all behind me now." Pause, long pause. "I... I had to do what I had to do, and I did, and that's all there is to it now. What else can I say? What can I do now? It was all done to push and steer you away from the edge anyhow, the very one that you were about to fall over..."

"So you-you, you mean you were there 'pushing, or pulling,' or whatever else you were supposed to be do-do... Doing, trying to steer me away from the edge! What edge, man? eh! What edge?"

"Some things are best left unsaid, Shad, and yes, you should be glad that too was for your good and... and for your safety."

"Well, what—ev—ver."

"Whatever? What kind of talk is this?"

"I got used to saying things like that quite a bit," said the shadow man, blaming these things now on his finger flips and his rolling hands between those rolling, folded-up palms of his. "...I-I picked it up on the job, you know? No, you wouldn't know. Things are different out there. Different from how they are here, but you wouldn't know that either, would you? No, I don't think so, you wouldn't."

"I ee, I do know quite a bit, Shad, more than you'd imagine, as a matter of fact, much more."

"Alright, alright, of course, you do, I got you. Yeah, right!" he whispered this part from behind his lips, teeth-tight, too. More pause.

"So, what really happened, Shad? Tell me. How come... how is it that you were not able to get the job done after all this time? I mean, you're 'the man,' aren't you?"

"If you had sent Bookie T along with me, you know him, my trusted weapon, and the master key? Like I didn't ask you to, same as how I didn't ask you to toss me in without even bothering to discuss it further. Like, sit down and talk to me about it, and ask me first before the bug-fit, or talk some more with me about it, before stuffing me into the purse with... Then you wouldn't need to ask me this now, would you, Nurse? (Spit). Together, Bookie T and I would have been up to the task. As we have always been. Both of us, together. It would have been done. But-but..."

"But what?"

"It's still just one of me, you know, up against all of them. As for them, they didn't come out empty-handed, no, sir, never. This leads to my next question: What are you going to do for me? Seeing that, as things are, and his... I've got nothing but nothing, and the quiz. I've got nothing in this whole kingdom but him. No, I mean, just me. What's now left of me, that is, and as you can see, it ain't even much on me. Lucky for you, though, you've still got everything going for you in the homely row. Despite everything, you're well on your way to getting your son back to the king, no? Come on, let's sing, like so. Sing along with me now: back to life, back to reality, back — "Cut that out, Shad, drop it, will you?"

"Okay, what can I say? Your son will be okay soon, though. Yes, and thank you for guessing, and even so, there are one or two more guesses left to go. Thanks again for that, and this, guess who this is? None other than yours truly: me, the Shadow man to be, as usual, and guess where I'll be when all this is truly over and done? Not with the new gal, no, not even one, not with any of them, but yes. In the shadows again, as usual... damned am I." Pause. "How is he doing, by the way? How much longer before he will be out of intensive care for the day?"

"Who, what? What intensive care are you...?"

"There you go again, gone, to the distant lands, there but not quite there. Do you know what I think? I think you are beginning to get a bit senile over here, or maybe you're tired and sleepy. Go to bed, man, and go p, p..." Pause. He had to hit the pause upon the bad-looking eyes of the king's looking glass, through the eye-bag. But, at last. "Look," he said, "I, me, people like me, like him, that one even, like them..."

"Don't point, Shad, you don't have to point at them, my friend."

"Okay, I hear what you say, but still. Look this way, just look at them across my thumb. Not my pointy finger this time, per se. But look at them, like this way, can you see them now? Those people there, look, they are just like me, and all the others out there that you may see. Those in the humanoid world spheres, too: we're not like you remember? We're not you, we're liable to expire... and even if by some special provisions one's time should be extended somewhat, as seems to be the case now with me and the little brat—"What? What was that?" "No, not to worry about little things such as that, it's just how we sometimes talk over there when we chat. But, as I was saying, even if our time should be extended somewhat, it won't be forever; we'll still all end up wasting away in the end, down the river. Only much slower than that, and them. But, but. What about that trucker? The one whose ashes I had was to sift my way through. Imagine that! I sat there all night, sifting through dusted remains of that mother of... You know, Mister Tucker. Like, like, doing it for you, for whatever reason. Doing the sifting shift to separate his burned remains and hence the residues of the Genodes, yes, them again. To separate them from those of his burnt-out rig and the cargo he was transporting, to go on and close out the gig. And, and… all this, in search of the long-lost Genodes? What is to become of him? And those? Then there were those daughters or guards of yours. Whichever they are to be found coming in after me through the doors, in fact, or going off on hidden scores, playing craps. Those wonder women who had shown up as if they were friends, but were not. 'For my good,' they had said. And what's up with all that, that thing, with me having to suffer the indignity of being thrown into prison for thousands of years, into infinity? Maybe more, like tens of thousands on the scores, and being made invisible to the eyes of those humanoids while I was in there and walking the floors, and by whom? By none other than your own 'brother', who, by the way. You never bothered to tell me about him before this day. How come? How come I never learned anything about that score, if you ever had a brother in the outdoors? Or daughters for that matter, and sisters, and, and… And how come? How is it that what's 'good for me,' always seemed to hurt so much on my back—"Hey! Watch it."

He shot the shadow man a scalding hot glance, like this. It stopped him in his tracks, off-balance, and hissed. "Watch your mouth, mister," he said.

"All right, all right: I'll wash my mouth, and-and, and go to bed."

Chapter 14: Out of Sight, But Not Out of Fire

He'd hitched a ride with him; he wasn't going anywhere in particular. Nowhere other than in search of the long-lost Genode pellets. The princely bit builder from college for the likes of kids to thrill her with it. So. While the over-confident, overly tattooed haulage truck driver dude was messing around with that driving bit. Shadow Needleman was there, concentrating his efforts on hacking the brakes on it. Yes, on the trucker's very own fast-moving big rig; he never knew what hit him, away from the crib. Speaking of hits. Shad had to whack that meowing pussycat hard at one point. Shut him up really quick on the joint. In his truck, on the seat on the passenger side of the vehicle, to the right of him, there it was, the carrying case for his cat-turned-pet-turned-traveling-companion, but-but, really now! Who the hell carries a cat around in a truck as a pet and traveling companion? Whatever happened to man's very own best friend and the family lion? Has he fallen so badly out of favor with the humanoid kind of a problem? Anyway, enough of them, I'd say. Back now to the task at hand, better days, and friends. Back to the story of the day, and the trucker man on the roadways, again. He saw the guard rails coming fast. Shad got out of there really quickly, departing through the glass. Yes, through the windshield of the big rig, since you'd asked, said speed. The fast-moving big rig plunged deep into a ravine and burst into a massive fireball, as you've never seen or would have cared to call. It just sat there and burned to ashes and all. Boy, didn't that baby burn? "Yes." All that remained of it when it was over and done, and after the smoke had cleared, back home, was twisted metal, debris, and ashes. Lots of ashes for me to go out and sieve, like these. "How in the world could one person ever get to be so darned lucky, though?" Asked the Shadow man while holding on to imaginary strands near the collar bow, and stroking pensively. "While some people were there busy," he continued, arguing with the king, you, and me. "...While I was there and very busy as a matter of fact, hopping across the universe for several millennia, on the rocks. Investigating many varied lifeforms and species, many other things like that, too, and the little gal pickney." Yes, that's who. He meant this as he was found to be doing these other things, like, while he was there doing what he did to those other species when he shouldn't have been. You know, and catching cats like these, all the while, scanning through many and varied dimensions across the seas, all in the never-ending search for the elusive Genode pellets, and trying to redeem them and then some. In the meantime, this one over-tattooed trucker was found there carrying around not one, but two pellets under his skin while on the rounds for you, including the BEACON on a string. "What's wrong with him?" Wow! What a dude! Well, guess who has got them now?

Ever since those days when the shadow man would have happened to pass by us. Cespedoran, too, before him, was on the bus as the story goes (and the chorus). They were here in the humanoid spheres and would have gifted the humanoid kind with the wonders of the tattoo arts and cultures. The king's Genodes, too, were carried in with him on the bow-ties for the vultures. "True." Allbeit unbeknownst to most of them, or all but us, no, not for me but... The pellets have been there among them. The Genodes have been there alongside humanoid beings throughout all of their memorable moments. Be it in their good times or bad times on the home end, the Genodes were there. In the times of the Crusaders, the Kings' Genodes were there. In the period of the industrial revolution, in the 18th century, the King's Genodes were there. In wartime, too, in the 19th and 20th centuries, yeah, the King's Genodes were there. As on down through to the age of global warming, the Genodes were always there. Where did it start for Shadow, though? Where will it end? Will it ever, like, end? I can't quite say for sure, my friend, I don't know. But naturally, wherever the Genodes were likely to be hiding in those times, Shadow would more than likely come calling and pulling on the chimes to try and haul them in; that was the reason and the rhyme, all hands in. He'd managed to find out that there were always trace copies of his lost Genodes almost everywhere he would go. Straightaway, he'd set out on the road to go and find them right away. The original ones, that is. Will he manage to get it done? Come along with the Shadow man, we've got things to do and places to go behind his van, yet, you bet. But, after a trek back from his trip up the Pole way, where he'd found the signal he was searching for one day. It led him smack-dab into the heart of the territories governed by, guess who? Yes, true. Still there, hanging on to the tusks of the boar from yesterday for stew. "Beware." None other than the beast-hunting, raw meat-eating, pellet-implanted hunter himself, roaming deep in the heart of a place looking a lot like the Polynesian mountainous region, walking the shelf. It was in those territories over there that Shadow found his long-lost hunter friend and his tribesmen again. He'd also discovered there that the pellet and the scanner that he had embedded into the hunter and his beast's carcass had more than served the desired purpose, and yet more for them and us. Not only did the scanner and those of the pellets that the hunter had attracted to himself, remain with the hunter and his community, the good part, but... Those pellets had multiplied thousands of times over (the bad part). "Shuts!" Shadow's task then was to go out and search amongst all those pellets to find his friends. The original ones, and what may be found coming again out of the hunter and his peoples who had eaten the dead and made ready-to-be-eaten beast bottoms too. Well, not so much those people themselves as they were to be seen living there at the time with you, but the corpse. The parts that were long gone through the corks, because for sure, the well-fed and then dead villagers would have been found to have gotten something to do with whatever was coming off the pellets through the trees and down to me and you today, no? I thought so... anyway, let's go astray, because, if any of the others, like the original pellets, should find their way into those regions and among the people living there. He must find those and get them home and away from here. He was lucky to find out, too, that the pellets that found their way into the structures of trees over the lifespan of their growth. Whenever those trees were burned, the pellets would be passed on through to the ashes' remains. All unchanged from their original forms, so that was where the Shadow Man started his next search. Welcome to the great, big, wonderful world of overly tattooed folks. "Ooch!" Since people are not trees, he had to think of a way to extract the Genodes out of them without killing or smoking them out like bees. So, that's how and when it happened. He whipped up a concoction of wood ashes from those regions with other pigments that he gathered from the elements around him. Adding and subtracting elements along the way, as was found necessary for him to go play and drown them, until he came up with the very first ever batch of tattoo ink, that way.

"If people could not only be made to become hosts and vehicles for the pellets," he thought, and sold it on the rest of the neat wheats we all like to eat, with broth. Not only were they able to preserve and cause them to multiply greatly, but people were found to be migrating from one place to diverse other places in those times, and along the tracks to hate me, with these signs. It had occurred to Shadow there and then that the humanoid body form would probably be the ideal agent to take the Genodes and the scanners throughout the universe, and hence, afford him a chance at tracking them down and retrieving the lost Kings' Genodes in the long run, from thence. There was a method to the madness and the wrong gnome, in a sense. "Sometimes it will take a lot of multiplication," he thought, to get to a simple subtraction, of sorts. Shadow then went out in search of his first guinea pig amongst the natives and went a bit further into doing his gig. To perform yet another experiment as he did. He found him there that evening, a young man, yes, he was, sleeping amongst the bugs, good for him. Good for the Shadow man, too. On into his slumber, the Shadow man went, competing with the bugs, clinging to his lint. In his first operation, he ran smack dab into a problem, a very big problem. Although he was careful to approach only sleeping subjects. Like this one, for instance, snoring and hanging on to his gold pets. Even though he was careful to apply liberally, his own Cekkoland type of numbing agent from the Goblets on each one's corpse above their knee. He'd notice that, as soon as he gets started with the operations, the subjects would wake up, not good for E's but... I mean, on him, but... Back to the drawing board he had to go: to find a solution, you know. That move led him to the creation of the first topical anesthetics, a specially formulated skin-numbing agent formulated to penetrate the skin for the relief of that or this sort of pain. And voila! The problem was solved, again.

Chapter 15: Back to the Future with Shadow

"I'm still none the wiser about those self-proclaimed daughters (those guards) of yours," said Shadow when the conversation resumed behind closed kingdom doors in the yard, oh. "And you haven't said anything against, nor in support of those claims. Are they, in fact, your children, your daughters?" Shadow inquired further about this from the king, with slap-swapping hands and laughter among them.

"How did you find out about that, I mean, about that part of them? And about who they supposedly are?"

"Answer the question, my friend, will you? And not with another question of your own, what has become of you? You're no different from your father now."

"Shad, I'm warning you, don't push it."

"Don't push what?"

"Your luck, don't push your luck too much. Or you might get—"Alright-alright, I hear you. I heard you the first time, too. I first met them when they showed up to bust in and burst me out of that god-forsaken prison. And you, yes, thank you for that." I do thank you for that if it was, in fact, you. Is it because of your doings, was that a given, my king? He whispered from somewhere within... I really appreciated it then, and I still do, so..."

"Wait, God-forsaken? God-forsaken? What kind of talk is this? What gods are you referring to here?" Hiss.

"No, no, this one is not yours, it's not for you. It's just a figure of speech, you know; a saying to get us through the beats to go, go. An earthly thing to do. It's not about you, no, it's not about us nor our gods. It's, it's, it's about them." There he goes, back-flipping his fists again, like so. It's about them and their gods, the other people, and their gods, that's who I'm referring to in this case, you know? Those other people over there in the yard and the "other" race. They've got their gods, too, you know, but... Anyway, let's go... astray. Laughs. Like I was saying... and still want Ted to say, sorry, I meant to say, wanted. The girls showed up on the day when I was busted out. Don't you get me wrong here, I was glad in the end that they showed up, but I almost crap my pants—"Wah... what, what's this, this kind of talk? Why does it keep on coming up like that?"

"Oh, sorry, I just keep forgetting." Please forgive me, my friend, Li King. Oh, man! Pause. "How was I supposed to know, though? How was I to know that you have all these other things going on, children, and brother, or brothers? How many are there anyway? When did this happen, all of this? When did it all happen?"

"That's my business and mine only, (hiss). We're talking about you here, mister man, and you alone, carry on, carry on with it."

"Okay-okay, I will, one day perhaps, but still." More laughs. "I, I was just about nearing the end of my rope; nothing seemed to remain for me; no hope of my ever getting out of there. Until that day in the morning way when it started to rain: there was lightning and thunder earlier that day, then came the rain, before there was to come, those smoking swords slashing through time and into my space as though... ugh, man, I mean, it was like, it was as if it was a hot knife through butter but, it was slashing through the but... I mean, through the bones and marrow of people from tomorrow. All this was happening while, as it were, the captain and his mighty men of war didn't seem to have even so much as a prayer in the form of a response to their assault. The sun was up in all its brilliant glory by then; it was as if they'd dragged it back in with them. I thought it was an army of over ten thousand strong and mighty men that had come out against us. Me included. But I was amazed to find that it was a company of three, just three unassumingly slender but very well-sculpted and firm-bodied female fighters like me. Well, yes, their helpers were there trailing behind them, well-dressed and cruising along like motoring bikers, and the crew was eyeing them. But it was just that small company that came out with them, and you, no? "No, not with me, but..." "I know, those warrior girlfriends of yours were, though," wielding smoking swords of might and mightier, at them. Conquering to conquer, everything. Well, again, let me try to explain. The girls were the ones wielding the swords; the others with them were almost yawning and bored. The most dreadful thing that I saw there in those assaults on the camp at that time was the zip-pity-zap lightning balls that they carried and would throw back at the guards. Even over the shoulders on what might have seemed to others like a retreat, on the go, as if they were going off somewhere to eat something in the yard, but no.

They would have done it like that every single time, you know. Which was good enough to get those frightened jailers scampering for cover, but they were never able to mount any form of military response. At least none that would have been good enough to withstand the fury of the lightning balls coming off them at once, so it seemed to this one. I thought I was going to be consumed in the wake of the furious feminine assault. But I was quickly scooped up and dragged away, kicking and screaming, even to a fault. I was picked up like prey, and swiftly taken away from this and that... from all the other places and times in the slot, which I'd estimated to be about another thousand years forward from that point, in humanoid terms and time measures. How long was it anyway? How long was I cast out there that day, in real terms?"

"Twelve hundred and three years."

"Wow!" said Shadow, sitting there in pensive reflection and sniffing the air, like so. "No further questions," he said. Long pause, from there.

"It took me another forty to fifty years, you know, human years, that is, yes." So continued the Shadow Man, starting rather slowly as you had guessed, again rolling his hands in his fists, and platting his fingers at the man like... like this. "...to realize that I was free, that I was delivered and set free from ever being under the bandage of those miserly jailers, and she. But my mind did not catch up to it quite as quickly, to that concept, you know. Not as it did to the wonders of those fighting girls, undressed to go for the failure, wish it had."

"And then?"

"And then, after those things. I looked out over the waters, and there it was, the loopy dopy wobbling thing riding the waves like dead bugs, occasionally raising its head as if to look above the water and then diving back down again despite the gaze. "Ugh!" Then up and down again, and yet again. It went on like that for days, gliding along on the water's surface. Spooky, spooky indeed was that one, oh yes, man, yes."

"Go on, go on, what happened next?"

"But—but, why are you not alarmed? What's going on here, Liam? Really? Do you know something about it, about that wobbly beastly thing?" Hmm. "Yeah! I'm humming a song to go sing for him, again." But after a long pause, Shadow continued stating his cause. "Things changed a lot over time," he said, "and four thousand years is a hell of a long time for changes to happen. For things to change and be replaced, and boy, did they ever change? Yes, yes, they did." Back to life on the home front, though, listen to him there telling more of the story back in Cekkoland, as it was to be heard continuing in there, and on the row.

"Can I get some shut-eye first? I mean, can I sleep on it? Oh, wait a minute, sleep? Never mind, eat, eat." Shadow dreaded the very thought of ever sleeping again, even though he was back in the comforts of home, sitting there and talking with his friend. He will never be comfortable with that routine again, not after what would have happened to him.

"You know, you're right," said the Shadow man on that same night, "You are the man, I mean, The King, sorry, sorry."

"You've got two options here, Shad; it's all up to you. It's up to you to choose which."

"I'm to choose one, now, you mean now? Right this minute?"

"Yes, peable-did-the-damned-lit man, yes." Now, King Liam was so disgusted at this, he clapped his hands down on his trousers with those kingly arms of his, which he always uses to enclose and arouse the alarm in others, such as her, and to get his move on, in bids. Yes. On the home front near the cribs, as it occurs.

"Okay, man, okay. Let me see. Choice number one is, I could go back out there as some sort of mortal human being, like, as a mortal man? Ugh, interesting that one is interesting indeed. I'd met some rather interesting folks out there, you know, seven — " "Seven?"

"Yes, seven of them, 'said Speed.' Seven women that I had met and gotten upset with out there, they're still to be found troubling my mind over here. Some want Ted to own me, some to stone me, and... Women whom I could have done things with, or done things to, or both."

"Don't you mean, women with whom you did things, way too many things? That wasn't the purpose of your trip there, you know, it was to

— "Yes! Yes! I know, I know, man, I know. This was meant to be light and funny here, but you... Nah, you wouldn't understand that one or two. So, let's leave it as is and move along, (the brook) with you." As you were saying... No, oh no, don't bother with that one, I smell trouble here, and it's like brewing beer."

"What? What's the trouble?"

"I'd rather not say, you wouldn't understand anyway. Hand me one of those beers, please. What's the other choice? Um, (gulp,) this is nice. I'm at ease."

"Well, you can do neither and stick with the status quo. In which case, that would make it three choices, wouldn't it?"

"Whoa! You mean, choice three is: let things continue as they have always been? Continue along the same path I've been going in Cekkoland for the past sixteen thousand years and counting, give or take a few of them? And continue counting your toes to ten, I mean, shoes, sorry. What's choice number two, again?"

"You could take a chance at running this place, now, tell me; how does that sound to you? Is this to your taste? How — would — you — like — that?"

"Take a chance at what? You mean, I could become like, like you, like, like, the king? What does it all entail? I mean. Really?" Shadow pondered these things in his heart for a brief moment, freely. But then, it hit him hard when the king interrupted the silence, again, it was golden — "There's nothing to it, Shad, it's not that hard. You can do whatever you want, even in the backyard, whenever you want to, like playing cards, even. On any given day, you may decide to sleep in, go window-peeping, bare-back beast riding, or you could go out fishing."

"...Fishing?" He swallowed hard at that thing, really hard. His stomach gave him a loop-a-do and threatened to give up his beer breakfast to the backyard and in the hardened view. Oh, Lord! "Fishing?" That's the last thing that Shadow would ever want to be caught doing again in his life. He doesn't want to do the fishing thing ever again, not after what would have happened to him.

Chapter 16: Oh! For Girl's Sake!

I saw them there, beauty beyond compare. I couldn't help myself, I had to stare. I knew they were sis, but then, they kissed... I mean, they kissed me. We were to have kissed, you know, eventually, and then it happened. With her hands outstretched, her thigh heaved up to strike the solid thing that had awakened me to life. A lively thing I never knew that I had before, or that I was capable of. I didn't even know I had it to give to a wife, even with all those incarnations under my belt. This time, for the first time, I felt this strange thing bubbling up from within my mind, right there and then. That was when I came to know what it meant to live, to really live, at last. "I missed you so much, all my life in fact," I mumbled through her breathing. Sneaking it in through her parted lips while she was looking at me from behind closed eyes, and deep-talking to me through the teething. A tight hand-gripping hold, on heavy breathing. But how could I have known all of this? It's as if I were mastering something I loved a lot, and was expecting to feast on the fat. Again, she kissed my face and threw flames like a blowtorch down my spine, and that was when it happened. It was my first time, but then again... She grew momentarily shy. Her face was buried in my tunic, next to my tie, as she gave me the top of her head, don't ask me why. I don't know, but, oh my! I breathed smoke and steam into each strand of her long flowing hair that received me, it was like burning in there and, and... That's when she bent over backward and lay down, sprawled out on her back, to the ground, her head took turns to the one side, then the other, as she moaned. "Crucify me," she said, and lied when she said it, then sent me to work and to bed it. I labored hard at trying to save her, but, as always, she's never dead, not yet. You don't know, man, and I hope no one will ever come to know just how beautiful that woman is; she's really, really something. I never knew it myself, not until I gazed up at her from that angle, from below the belt. Nobody taught me anything about this, but I one-up the practice. I fumbled at undressing her with my trembling hands while, like a cat, she moaned and purred. With my mouth, with my eyes, with my tongue, my imagination. With my, my, my, oh my! With me, even with everything. I had to hurry to get to that place between Cornwall and Surrey. No, not to worry, or you'll be sorry. Her lively, freshly rain-wet centers in Half Way Tree were centered and focused... on me. Then, she fused into me, like glue. Look at you! Look. "Look at me," she said, "look at me some more so that I can feel the caress. The ravaging of your eyes and then your head, rest. Hold up your head, man, and look. Touch me, touch me, yes, there, and cover me with your skin, and your locks of hair. Kiss me, kiss me there again," she said, and... That was when I kissed her, there and then, and banished the talking from her end. And, and... My heart flew away. And, and...

"And his mind was quick to follow. That's what he's trying to say, my good fellow, but..." Shad had been searching everywhere since, but couldn't seem to be able to find it again, his mind now on the mince. She outrightly stole it from him. But who's complaining? Surely, not him. "I never understood the mortal touch, like, the spoken words and such, until I found her and tasted her mouth, and her tongue spoke up." I had to hunch slightly forward to try and mitigate the swelling of the crowd in that region of the woods, you know, out of town, as we went along the way to go, taking it home, and her? She did turn at least once to glance at the ballooning crowd, in that self-same region of the park in the halfway-tree city, near Mountain View Road. I could have sworn that I heard her gasp, "...Uh, woo." But alas! I could have been wrong, at last. I pushed my overactive halfway pointer, you know, look, my center stage is now near the most likely joint of hers. I pushed my way hard at the half-open door. She opened up the door a little more. She moaned and groaned, and then. You'd never believe what happened. The floodgates were flung open from within me, again. Then a million years of pent-up alien energy came flowing through. Unabashedly, just like you, the bands started to play. The sweetest music ever for you, I'll dare to say. The latest greatest hits of the day. "Coming to you off my numb —"Your number one DJ, right?" "Yay, say it that way. If you like." I slid my hand up under her dressing room, and up her smooth sides. She gripped my handling moves as if dismounting from the horse after the ride. I was (at the time) busily watching over her, protecting her from harm, as it occurred. I felt the nipple spout under my fingers and almost died from the alarm. Right there and then, from the warmth inside, spilling over the mile end. Would I ever have lied, my friend? I reached out, found her hand, and led her to my place on the new land. The mountainous regions of the estates. It was new even to me, but it was mine. She wasted no time directing traffic towards her summer destination, down the line. Then, she rolled me over, and Paris kissed me there, with the mouth-like spout that she keeps out of sight, but not out of my mind. "Beware!" Not anymore. She can no longer keep some things hidden behind closed doors. Not from me, these, or any other such hallowed shores, nearer to the raging sea, of yours. "See?" "Yes." Look, she reached out and took further control of things, this thing, even. She has a way of taking control of such things, of everything, in the evenings, and keeping those very things happening, just like that. But then again, relax, because... We took a shallow turn on the inside route and sucked moisture and hot air inside the booth, like a greedy sinkhole, and swore. I was smitten good and proper once more, and even after... Like, after we could finally stop. I knew right there and then that I could not, I mean, I would never be the same again, ever. Spend time walking in the other person's shoes, my friend and brother. Mine, even, and others. Spend a little time living their lives, witnessing their struggles, on the wrong side of the knives, even. Feeling their pain and their hardships. As well as all the other "hard" things that we as people over there have always had to endure, on the yard ships. You won't have to worry about such things over on these hidden shores. There, though, walking shoes can easily be yours. Those things are plentiful there. So, come on, come with me, let's go over there in the Bentley, and walk in them, experience them, and see. Come and see all these things with me. As well as love and passion. Passion for life even. Then and only then you might begin to understand this, and that. These things are there on the lot tory pot, my friend, never forget that fact, one, or ten. Her eyes were making me out to be a liar, a-burning me from deep within, oh, the desires... Which was what inspired and stirred me from the get-go. "You liar." "What?" "Never mind that." Stirred me into life, even to a glow. But we would have been gone by the next day, tomorrow. We had to both go away and repent because we had sinned, you know, yes. We'd transgressed some sacred things by our doings, I guess. So, we had to go. Some of us, rather reluctantly so, you know. Like dragging our feet, heels, and toes. But we would have been back because we would have remade ourselves a lot by then. Our identity, even, because of all the ghosts of the past, and our many wild acts of the evening. But alas! Believe him, upon my return, things began to happen, the fire began to burn again, fast. "Fast, those types of things were happening in our language class, but..."

Tomorrow at this time, she will be laying him to rest. Her father? He was the best. As for me? What does she know about me? Does she even know that I know these things, still? Life goes on for some of us, though, for the evil ones mostly so, and so it would seem. But as for me and all the others like me, as seen here in these dreams... Hmm, yeah! I'm here humming out some things for them, again. As these and other such things were to turn out, those women were well-trained. "Yes?" "Yes, they were highly trained women, by all the shouts and many acclaims." In the many and varied things that were to be blamed on their names. Not only because they wield a mighty sword, as was the regular everyday word of their lords, but they could also wield the power of many worlds, at the wards, even. Some agents from another world were soon to find out, and many were the powers they wielded at evening, with every battle shout. Power as a force of light, for instance, against the ever-present powers of darkness of the night, and the kings' sons. As for the men, those men over there. Many have gone insane from so much power that they wield to try it, I hear. This Shadow man, he too was drawn into it, yes, it was by this much power that they were driven to a fit. As for them, like those standing by the doors, and looking in. Some of the other men over on the shores, can-can, can you see them? "Yes." They, too, would degenerate into becoming instruments of darker powers, like you. Something that will probably become an issue for them in their final hours, it's true. For everyone, even, and starting soon, even in the shower. Both the present and the future together seem to weave uncertain fates for these individuals. Things seemed to happen and move along in mysterious ways over there for these girls on those shores and tides, Al. But things are not always what they seem. These fighting girls weave webs across the doors, and wield their swords as the girls will, I mean, yes, in these parts, and in dreams. As it was to be seen happening in all other such things. These strong female, leader-type characters were creating havoc for many in the process, and in their hearts, no less.

Sedalie Newman is the leader of the pack as it stands over there; she wields a great amount of power and a mighty sword, too. Even as the wisdom of the group, to scare, and to sail on down the line, and get through. But as for Elsie? Elsie is a leader in training for me. Sedalie is the kind of girl for that sort of job, and to remain in. She was my girl from the get-go, but I had to settle for Elsie, you know. Because she said so. Elsie said so, that's why, okay, bro? My! Oh my. The whole realm will soon be ruled by a strong queen if Sedalie Newman is to have her way with these things. She will soon reign. To be succeeded one day by Elsie, again we say, maybe. Heaven, or somewhere else, perhaps. Let's stick with heaven here, just so we may be able to compare these bottled beers on those shelves of her pops. Heaven helps them if that day should ever come. I can't think of a more evil female in these exalted realms than Elsie, yes, that one. Not so with the men, though, as you can see. As opposed to how it is with her, as in Elsie. In these parts, it had long been a given that the men were in charge. So, there was nothing for them to prove to anyone, nor to improve. "Now, come on!" "The men were in charge of everything," they say. That was a given — okay? In theory. It won't be long before something (or someone) is going to sneak up their backsides, though. To come in and institute a new normal in these lands, on the go. Take it from a shady stranger like this one... "You mean, Shadow Needleman, no?" Yes, the Shadow Man, even. Yet, there are strong and delightful male characters over there in those lands. As in some high command, too, no matter how they had gotten there to stand with you. They were there, yes. From some very well-abled custom keepers up, or down, to the current chief himself, and his son, Carmie. To an extended belt and looping the runs, calmly. As for the guards and agents tasked with keeping things in order on the home end, there, for me? These are still very capable and well-loved men in general spheres to see and spend on David's tea. The chief's son, though, that same Carmie bro. who had lain himself down to sleep once upon a long, long time ago. Long, according to Earth standards, as such things were to go. He has not woken up again since. Not in terms of him maturing and getting himself in a state of readiness to assume leadership of the region, no. His "kingdom" is hanging in limbo. Things are weighing in the balance and are ready to go. But Carmie is sleeping, bro, still. Most of all, there are some grave concerns to come into the call, because so far? Trouble is brewing over there on the late show calls, coming in from behind those very doors hanging on the walls. Want to see more, yes? "Yes." Well, look. See that, fellow Seymour? One of the chief warders and gatekeepers, the current stewards of the training institute, and the entire security apparatus in and around those parts of the river? He's being closely watched and scrutinized under orders from the chief, of course. But as for him, Seymour doesn't even know that thing. Some sort of "leader and warder-in-chief" is he, at the heart of him, but as it is in life, in our lives even. The forces of good and evil are always working; they're often at odds with each other. Often cross-purposed, and can even be found to be under different orders than the conventional chorus, sometimes. Like, the children of light, and the children of darkness. As well as various other kingdoms and peoples who are always pulling wills one against each other like hornets. But all are against the weevils near the rats' nest. They all seemed at some point in time to be becoming threats, one towards the other, even now, ask the brother if you don't believe ours, yes, report. So, the question for us to ponder now is this: Will it go on? Can it go on like this, for how long? I can't say that it will, or even if it won't. I don't know, man, not yet. I would have wondered about it. Like, if the dark power could have ever been defeated over there. I do hope so, I swear. The plot will take many twists and turns. Only some may be resolved in the end, and fairly so, for all concerned.

Randolph, the chief, would have worked himself to death to provide for his family, to eat. And yes, for Evette too, yes, her, as it is, and me, even. In a back-handed way, from behind the door, sneaking in. For his beloved daughter, though, mostly so. The daughter of the evening, pardon me. However, a dark secret from his past seemed to be the driving force behind his need for such revenge. Against everyone, she meant, against him even, yes. The Shadow man, not Steven as you'd guessed, on unanswered questions. Elsie loves her family in truth, but feels as if she'd been cheated out of her youth. She's harboring some dangerous and explosive secrets of her own, and now... After her vile encounters with this man, the Shadow Man, a wild one from the outside of their world and beyond. Her troubles have now been multiplied a thousandfold. No, oh no, not as in, the folding of the arms, no. But the other one, made of gold and woven yarn, now goes... She was putting in a lot more time between her sleeping place and mine. But that was just for a short time. "Are you a hitchhiking kind of person, Shad?" Asked some of them over there, steaming mad. "Think again, think of getting a life before you go wanting the next one to have, and a wife, out of the bag." This, they meant in the same way as the melodious sounds coming out of the bagpipes, and then, wanting the next one too, because it's nice. None other than this same one. Who? Else, yes, she, as in Elsie, for you. And me...? Back home, though, there was another plan, but Shad was none the wiser about it. "Oh, sheet! Don't do it," said the snitch to a nosy little witch. But still, this; it had taken him way too long to get it done, and the edge had fallen off that one, yes, off his game. It was time to pull him out and call him home, again, so here it comes.

Chapter 17: The Shadow Problem Again.

"We must do something about this Shadow problem," they'd said, to one of them near the head on the far end of the bed, "...and fast." So, they went into the lab again to finish the task. Or more like, he was sent in, yes. Smokey was sent into the lab to do the job, and out came the new and exciting BDV. Who was he? And, and, who was the "we" of whom they spoke, there? Good question, with answers to hear, yes, man. The king would have summoned yet another assembly; it had taken the Shadow man way too long to get the job done by... as said, me, no? "Oh! You mean...?" "No, but..." The king's patience was wearing thin on that one. The last time he'd gone in to check up on Shad, he did not like what he saw. He wasn't very happy to be glad, because instead of getting closer to finding them and bringing the Genodes home. Shad was found to be there experimenting with some strange ideas and carrying on with the wrong gnome, my good friend. This seemed to the king and his advisors at the time to be running quite contrary to the norm and to the chances of accomplishing the task at hand; the real kingdom's task, yes, that one. Even after all that time, Shad had not gotten his hands on more than just a tiny portion of the pellets. Even those were then scattered abroad again, by way of the experiment he was found fiddling around with. Furthermore, according to the king's views of things from behind those kingdom doors. He was also found to be getting himself drawn way too deeply in with humanoid kinds, to be of optimal use to the kingdom and the task at hand, anymore. There were a lot more of such things, too, according to the reports that were coming running into them from you. It didn't take them very long this time to decide to pull him out and recall him home. So, Smokey was given the green light to go and "Make ready" the next agent in line for deployment into service that night. He promptly went and did just that, but then came this. "What? The fight?"

"No, he was protecting his fist, that's right."

"Oh! Yes, you're right, but..."

Smokey would have seen this as his chance at re-establishing contact with his extra-secretive "Toad" agent. The one he had not heard a word from in ages, since his deployment. Well, not quite. But that was how it was beginning to look and be seen to his longing eyes at night, that's what we all meant, you see, that's right. What do you know about traitors and why they do what they do? Love, probably? Even in the Cekkoland ways of looking at such things and viewing you and me? Well, maybe. The Shad problem was exhausting resources and (seemingly) not producing the desired results as they'd wanted. So, they had to come up with fresh ideas. That's how the Shadow Man was to get pulled out of combat, and a new agent got sent out in his place. The agents were never alone, although none of them knew that fact, but... but. "Here we go again...." If it wasn't for the bad types of luck, that is. Hadn't it been for this type, there would have been none for him to write home about that night. Because they were to show up there again, while the Shadow man was still wandering around in the wilderness, my friends. They had to shoot him unconscious because, at the time, they were unsure if he would have been able to survive the journey home to the kingdom on the ride with them, and fast. This was based on the condition he was found in at the time and the probable cause. Like, the fight he would have been likely to put up if he were not a willing participant in the operations and the flying part. He'd degenerated from being the sharp and capable agent they had sent out to do a high-stakes task. Based mainly upon the confidence that the kingdom had placed in those, of course, yes, his several abilities were desired over yours, who had asked? However, who, or more like, "what." What he has become as of late, and the state he was found to be in at that time, and place, begs a lot of them to ask whether he would have been able to pull it off. On this approach, Shad saw them coming in and took note, yes. He was ready to go out and toast his longtime friends from the dominion. He tilted his head backward and looked up through the leafy canopy of the trees in the forest, where he was at the time, seated idly by, looking up at them, and crying. He knew who they were; the prison bust was still fresh in his mind as it occurred. However, he had no idea why they would have been coming back around these parts so soon again, this time. Relatively speaking, from within, his chimes. He was not afraid, but he should have been. If only he'd known what it was that was about to strike him squarely, in the very heart of his pain, Leigh. The most painful spot of them all, yes.

For him, for all of them, those Cekko people, again. The Cekko people may be the kind who majored in the dying thing. Or more like the not-dying thing, yes, their pain tolerance level is the wonder of every other kind of people throughout the whole universe, and beyond. But the same is true of the nature of the pain they often have to go through and endure, without medications. How was Shad supposed to know that this was his day to face that most dreaded of all the Cekko vices, off the girls? He was out cold and foaming at the mouth before he knew what it was that had hit him, away from the world. Just one shot from one of those lightning bolts was all that was needed for the job. The jolt of medicine came out of them, you know, then came the sobs. A special type of lightning bolt load of saline was what they'd given to him. I mean, the type that was not designed to kill and destroy the man. Even though he was a super-agent from over there in Cekkoland, as he was known. But to render him incapacitated to the extent that he would have been out of it enough to be cooperative under their hands. Malleable even, as a clown, I mean, even as a toy. So now he's back, and, oh boy...

Lost in Summary. In the beginning, there was Shad, and some overshadowing, too, as we remember it, from that evening through. There came a day when all the elders and chiefs were summoned to the palace. To meet up with the king and his chief ministers at the old address was what they were promised. One by one, they came in through his gated doors, as was the custom even, and more. Liam was sitting in the royal chair, yes, but he was at it again, biting his fingernails and pretending not to be. Popping his knuckles too, no, not like me, but there he goes a-popping; pop, pop, pop. It's heard of him doing that a lot before, like, whenever he's troubled, upset, or insecure. Fear was not a factor in the mix in such matters, no. "He was never afraid," so they all said. "But, just not yet." "Probably, mi bred." After all, he had never been where the Shadow Man had been before the fall. Nor has he seen any such thing as him, not at all. So, no. They didn't know at the time what it was all about (for the most part); they didn't know that the vile one, Cespedoran, had grabbed the Genodes on the way out back. But it was quickly figured out; they had all gone down the river track to pick up rocks. Then, a high-level meeting was convened to plan and strategize for the safe return of said most valuable kingdom treasures back home and to deliver them to the throne. After the fallout of Cespedoran, I mean, he fell through the hole that had opened up on the floor beneath the feet of the big man. Beneath the feet of him and his cronies alike, that evening. "I'm weak!" he complained while lying on his face before the king. Yes. Just like that, and just like that, he was gone. As were all his friends and cronies, they were no longer their problems over there in the immediate environment of the kingdom on the stone ends. That was for sure, not in the place they'd called home. But the Cespedoran problem was far from over and done, and everybody there knew all that was to be known about that one. Other fallouts were to come too, soon. By way of that very same hole, even, you just wait and see who, whom. What they didn't know at the time was the full extent of the damage his departure was about to have on the kingdom and the inhabitants of the highest realm. It was quickly figured out, though, that the Genodes were all gone. Then, a high-level meeting was convened to plan and strategize for the safe return of said most valuable kingdom treasures back home. The prince, Bauctnumboulei, was a baby when it all started to unravel, and it began to happen that way. "Just days old in humanoid terms and time measures," I heard them say... No, no need to remind us, we've not forgotten about that part of the argument, yet. So, it's our pleasure, we'll now go and show it to them, no? "Yes, let's do this." He hadn't grown more than an easy span of his father's right hand since those events, nor up until then. He was not expected to get any bigger than that either. Not until the Genode pellets are found and returned home to the kingdom, so that the proper rituals and applications may begin to take place in the boy's life to aid him in his development to become the next one, and bright. Yes, the next king, just like his father Liam. Everything is at a standstill for him, seemingly, until then. The meeting dragged on for days, weeks, even months. By the time they'd managed to come to some consensus and agreed upon a plan of action that evening, against us.

Everyone present was barely even present anymore, in terms of the levels of wellness and alertness needed for them to function properly on those Cekkoland shores. The edges had even started to fall off some of the super-sharp wit and tenacity of some of them. They were all tired and beaten, so I was to hear. Even in Cekkolandee terms and languages, so to speak. Even in those other Cekko things, as prescribed for their weary feet, too. The effect was the same. They needed to get some rest, by any other name. That, though, was mistake number one for Shadow. "Or was it, wasn't it number two?" "Um..." Anyway one might ever wish to look at it and calculate it through, it was a mistake of gigantic proportions for him to chew on. For the things he had to do before his time came around to go to the new land, even. When the Shadow Man finally woke up from his slumber, an awful lot had changed around him. Which was not very good for him to believe in (the numbers), or was it? Oh sheet! Look at this... Shad has been dreading the whole idea of sleep since then, even while walking the earthly realms. Look! Over here. Can you see him through this thing? There, look! There he was, in another world. Somewhere far away from the place he'd long called home, and from his Cekkolandee girls, too, as they were known to him and you. But he was there with a mission to find and return the lost Genodes home to their rightful place. A forcefully imposed mission it was, like, just shoved in his face, like a mug. He knew immediately afterward that that was his task. Because that was, in fact, the very centerpiece of the extensive discussion they were all a party to before dawn when he went to sleep. No decisions were made there and then, so to speak, as to who it should have been, like, who would go, and when, Mom. But Shadow knew enough about such things and how they work to have known that he would be the chief suspect for such a task. Come on. This is due to his standing and position in the hierarchy of the kingdom's security apparatus, and how such high-level missions were set up. As well as his "let's go" kind of mentality, his "let's do this" motto, and work attitude. Never would he have imagined, though, that they would have blindfolded him and cast him headlong into the role, without even so much as discussing it further with him first. At least, that part of it, if nothing else. But he was in, and there was no way out for him, other than the way out from among them. More or less, like what a Nike type of fellow might have said at one time or another from behind a shout, yes; just do it, go get it done, and bring it home, Shad. But, you must be mad! "What kind of people do things like that?" Shad was heard to have wondered sometime later and reacted. What sort of mind would have conceived such a thing, like, to send a man away on such a mission without the benefits of his weapon? Nothing in his hand except some hard, bone-dried sin ting fei nyam? Sorry, I meant to say, some well-preserved silver nuggets to eat, okay? He had his weapon in his hand when he got back home, as was the custom for him to do so in Cekkoland. But now? Yes, look at him. He's back here in Cekkoland now, and sitting down beside the king, somehow. He's getting more and more upset just thinking about it, yes, this thing, his friend Liam is begging him to..., no, not begging but telling. He's telling him to quit. "Forget about it, and sit, sit down," he said. But he won't. "Sit down, servant. Sit down, nuh."

"You know, you know I can't sit down," so replied Shadow's disobedient jawbone. "Sit, I say. Sit on it, okay. Whatever "it" is. Ugh, too darned unruly you're beginning to be. Wherever you pick it up, it will do you well to take it back and away from us. From me, of course, and go put it back down."

Meanwhile, look at him, that Smokey being. Smokey is a cunning being, an astute and very wise individual, and the chief of defense staff is what I mean, mi original... He would have known first-hand that Shadow would not easily accept this task and run with it. Or did he? Did he even know the sheet? Did he know him that well? The records would seem to disagree that they fit that cell. But he knew enough to have known for sure that if there's someone in the kingdom who's more than able to get it done, it would have been that same Shadow Needleman. The noble name for someone such as him, a leader, that kind of person he was. So, why bother? Why bother with all that rigmarole of negotiations up the ladder? Just blindfold the guy and toss him over the border. That was exactly what he did when he got home to the inn on the water. But then again... This same Smokey, of whom we speak, is a chief in the kingdom of the KD's. He's a ranger, or something else like that, no stranger to the facts. A priest, maybe, or something to do with stirring the pots to sweeten the tea. Yeah, Leigh. He oversees all strategic and military issues as they relate to the welfare and security of the royal family. He's the one who prepares all the agents for deployment, as well, not me. Whatever the task might be for them to do, as it is now in this case. The searching out of the long-lost Genodes, for example, my kids, and as to how blending the iced tea under his nose is to go on the give. It's he, yes, him. It's Smokey himself, not the king, who oversees such things. He sometimes does the hands-on work of preparing all these agents, too, and beverages in the basement on which to sip while they bite and chew. But he has a secret or two of his own, and ambitions somewhat unknown. There will be a revolt or some such thing in the kingdom soon if they're not very careful in hanging on to the throne on the moon. In the meantime, there's a young man whose life is hanging in the balance and is almost dying. Somebody is going to have to step up to the plate and bat like a champion to help him out. Or he might end up in another state of being, in another race. Or even to become an earthling away from this place, perhaps. "Such a waste," if you'd bothered to ask. Shad must help him get out of this situation. If he can, anyway he can. That young man should have been king already, and reigning in the Cekkoland realm, but...

Chapter 18: A Is for Assimilation

Unlike how things were to go with the Shadow Man. He was forcefully pushed out and into the task, by way of sleep in slumberland. Beahon was put through the A-chamber to prepare him for his entrance into the humanoid world, as a newborn baby. As is the regular custom over there, no "maybe." The plans and preparations for each agent's voyages were mostly secretive and covert. But there was always another top-level secret plan, but of course, known only to one person and suspected by another, Shad, perhaps. "Or two, Shad's friend Liam, no?" "Possibly true, my pops, go." But, each of the other agents was also trained and prepared according to the several entries they were making into the humanoid world, including the secret agent, no, not the girls. But the one sent in at... or somewhere around the same time as Shadow was sent. He was always somewhere around the next bend, doing his sort of secretive work to pay the rent, as such things are known over here; not a red cent. But known only to one, and by one person on the ground: the head cop, the chief priest and and... This agent took the form of a toad. It was rarely seen full-blown at any time or by any of the other agents while out on a mission on the road. Well, any but Shad, Shadow would have caught a glimpse of it a time or two, or even more. Much more than me and you, for sure, well, perhaps. His curiosity was piqued enough to have pulled him deeply in at one point, much deeper than any had foreseen or planned for in the joint. Good for him, good for them. Good for the king and his son. Not very good for Smokey, though, in the long run, nor for his secret toady agent at the end game, and down the road. But Smokey doesn't know that yet, hasn't deciphered that new code. He hasn't seen or heard from this particular agent in quite a while, or regained contact with this super-secretive agent again since, you know! Like, since somewhere around the time of Shadow's return home to the precinct, in a high-riding style, we think. Well, not too much longer for you to wait, Smokey. You'll be seeing something soon, like me; quote me. Other agents might have seen the secret agent while it was out on the route. But it saw them all, yes, that brute. Toady saw all of them and would have been "in the know" about everything they were out there doing. Up until that point, when he'd opened his big mouth and spoken. Spewing spit around the town end, and choked, then, things began to happen, bad things for him. After the initial operations that Shadow would have performed on the thing, the toad was rendered vastly incapacitated and wandered listlessly in the wilderness, Kid. It was left up to Bautnumboulei himself, though, in his earthly persona below. He caught up with it again, and upon instructions given to him by his father, King Liam, with help coming to him from the potion that he was given at the same time, and by the same individual. He'd managed to render the toad agent as lifeless as the little lazy gal and would have gone on to work his magic on mummifying the creepy jumping thing. As was to be seen happening up there at his temporary workshop in a wilderness setting, he tucked it away in his carrying sack and lugged it around with him for several centuries in his backpack, sir. Hanging on to it for decades or years more, until he met with agent Beahon in another wilderness meetup setting, and handed over the dead beast to him for transportation home. Back to Cekkoland and the throne. Beahon, too, ended up lugging it around for several years, like you. Decades, even, before his liftoff from an ice platform somewhere in a place looking like the Austrian Alps, in a mushrooming cloud of steam, smoke, and fire. Homeward bound towards Cekkoland, on the higher. Now, follow along as we try to fill you in on the rest of the story as planned. "Liar."

Look. He's grinning sheepishly now and sliding in. Into the narrow inner channel of the chamber, I'm riding in, all the while defiling his shaky and trembling...something, as I'm able to remember, okay? I'm joking. Smokey is being himself, as smooth as an eel, as usual. He's there administering special services to Beahon's... Look. He's patting the young man reassuringly on the back of the shoulder to ease the tension. He's rubbing his head now, ruffling his long, shoulder-length, dirty brown hair, as it was said, Wow! Did he not push the boy in a bit there? More or less like a New York City cop would? I could have sworn that he did, and swear at it, but that Smokey dude, sure is smooth. A very cool ruler, is he. Look, Beahon is now fully committed to the task. Whether or not he wants to, he's in and up to his — ask me no more questions about the other points of the plan, through. Is this the point of no return for him and you? Well, whatever, look. He's securely in now; there's no going back for him from here. Wow! Beahon D Vaille has really progressed a lot, and in the shortest amount of time possible at that. He'd had a severe case of cluster phobia not too long ago. Go ask the Huxtables, they should know. But thanks to the masterful job done by the master himself, Master Smokey. Thanks to him, Beahon is now ready to enter into the belly of the very beast that he'd feared the most of all in the beginning. There, look at him squeezing in. In he goes, without even so much as a single sighting of a wayward, solitary bead of sweat on his brow, or anywhere over the nose. "Wow!" If they should ever meet again, Beahon would have earned his badge and many stripes off him, well, perhaps. Smokey does not doubt that this will be a good one, too. Just like all the rest of the very well-abled agents whom he's had the pleasure of knowing, and you. Yes, of course, he knew about you. It was like, just a quick "hi!" and "bye" with him when running into you. No, not I, I wouldn't have lied and sinned — "Against who?" "You, no?" "Yes, true." Not in such important things, though. Smokey would have trained and sent them out on the mission field before, with well-streamlined instructions to them and him, for sure, of all his kingdom's things to do. Things he called chores.

Chapter 19: The Comings and Goings of Beahon.

Beahon was a boy then. Well, not in the same sense as every other boy around the town end. But boy, anyhow, as they are known over there on his homely side of town, to blow-wow. He has been through a lot of different things and has gone through many different stages in his life thus far. That's not in the same sense as every other person you may run into on the streetcar, either, or even at the karaoke bar, Freda. What, or who, he may become next, though, wasn't the number one question on his mind at this point in his existence, to go. He was suffering from a chronic case of recurring Deja vu syndrome, you know, that feeling of having been here. Or of having seen that thing there before. Has he been around these parts before? One might wonder, yes, I know, you're there wondering about those same things too, even now. But run along home somehow, go, yes, I'm talking to you, no? "No." "Okay." Blow. Beahon was that type of personality; he, too, had been around quite a bit in his time to have been able to see. Was he here before, on this dusty pile of earth ore? One way to find out for sure. Hop on, we've got things to do and places to go, not too far away from your door, no? Beahon D Vaille, or BDV, "The whiz kid" as he was known in the body art community in those days, even though he was still a teenager, and was nursing a new phase. He was "The man." The biggest tattoo man in town. He was at that stage in his life where he was beginning to discover new things. Things such as sports, music, and girls like you, Musette. Among other such fun things to do in the humanoid world. "You bet." Just, for example, we're using this sample, my girl. Angela was a fun girl, bubbly and outgoing to a fault. With just enough "crazy" to have been tantalizingly interesting to the heart. Her innocent charms and beauty could make any boy's (or even grown men's) heart dance on hot asphalt, on the stone ends. The size of his heart's eyes detested even the notion of restful sleep in her presence, at her feet, even. Oh! for the joy of being with her, of loving her, holding her, having her. They'd met at a spring break jam on the waterfront earlier that year. He'd by then lost all that he had ever known and cherished of who he was, up until that point, my dear, seemingly so. It was his first-ever trip away from home, too. His first trip going anywhere without his loving parents hanging on his arms, with you. Or they might have some other grown-up to chaperone him out, as they would sometimes do, of old. This means: He was growing up, yes, he was coming of age. Any day now, Beahon the whiz kid will be a fully grown man and out of the fold-up cage, mi old man. wow! Some folks over there had quite a bit of trouble with that concept, though. So I was told when I was to hear them say so, "And why is that?" you'd asked. It's because when it comes to the levels of maturity between Beahon and his folks, his "parents?" Most people who knew them would swear on their mother's life near the rear-ends that, as it is. The son's levels of maturity, as a kid, seemingly, far outperformed those of the parents, both put together to fit with ease, in these. Some had even gone as far as to say that it would seem as if the boy had been walking this earth long before their times, and ours too. Ugh, now chew. Then, put that in your pipe and smoke it, if even for a minute or two. Will you? The connection between Angela and Beahon seemed ready-made in alien heaven. Or hell. Or in some other far-off lucky chambers, such as that tiny cell, well, perhaps. "Who's to tell?" Asked another rotten old cop. According to what's happening now, on these paths, or not happening, I'd assumed such and such. Or it might have been somewhere else that it was smelled. Somewhere, such as over there, where everything always happens to turn out just right, all the time. They would have struck it off from the get-go, belying the usual signs like so, you know. "I think I like her a lot," he said, even before he'd managed to hit the hot bed and pull the pillow up under his head. But what did all of that mean? He had no concrete idea. None whatsoever, "What should I do next?" he wondered in a text and posted it out to his address list. He seemed to be coming up short on the scales, and fast from behind doors too, even yours, little miss, no? "True." "I know." He was trying to measure up in weight to the expectation levels around people in general and girls in particular, and not knowing why, he wanted to thrill her (seemingly so). But then, one night, after leaving me, despite it, they were to have kissed. Well, it was her, it was Angie who'd done it, yes, blame it on Angie because she would have pushed the limits and kissed him, too hard on round lips. Right there, on purpose, sis, not on the miss to hurt us, kids, no. He saw the lights, right there and then. Of a different kind of star at night, amen. Or more like, a multitude of different stars, popping up and out from there wherever you are, no? "No." Okay, whatever you say, I'll go away, one of these days. But the stars were popping out from everywhere else; it would have seemed so anyway. Something was different; he could feel it. They were getting really close by then, and Angie was more than ready to take the relationship to the next level and beyond, to reveal it all, to Beahon. But as for him, that Beahon friend of hers, wasn't budging. "Oh, come on! In." It's like he didn't quite get it. Even with the nudge and me-ber suggesting fits, on kisses. Or was it her? Angie wasn't sure, so she was wondering. "Is it me?" She was asking this when I got in and overheard her inquiry. She wasn't sure, but she had to find out, so she took it to him by way of the mouth, to begin. The doubts have all been settled now, and there's no more possibility of anyone else getting in between those two. No, not even you, a blow-wow.

Beahon was an only child, an adopted only child. Not only that, but no one around those parts seemed to know for sure who he was. Like, who were his kinfolks? "Who is his next-of-kin?" They would often joke about it, or ask the neat wheats, from whence he'd come. They were heard asking about these things even while jogging the run. They found him there that time in a basket on the front doorstep of mine, no, not mine really, but of a church where I'm trying... "Yuh feel mi?" Crying out his throat, of course. Pink, cold, and shaking like a leaf up above the earth. Thrown out of the fouled-up foliage and suspended for unruly behavior, perhaps. Left hanging out there by the savior, probably, my pops. To wither and fall from the tree and die on everybody but me, that's all. "Oh, my!" All their efforts to find his next of kin would have turned up short; they found nothing that could link him to anyone, anywhere around those parts, not even as a start. He became a ward of the state. He then bounced around from one crappy old foster home to an even worse excuse for another. Hope, though, would have sprouted triumphantly when he was later put up for adoption and was adopted by your brother, The Fatman, no? "No, that man is not my brother, but this one." The couple who finally got him as their very own son were delighted beyond all measure to get one. Like, a kid of their own to bring home. They'd tried for many years to make a baby of their own. When all else failed, they had to turn to adoption as a last resort, they'd said. It was their last hope of parenthood, and bringing one home that was good. Strangely enough, they'd managed to come up with and given him a name not quite unlike the very name he had before; Beahon D Vaille it was, for sure. The papers were all signed, sealed, and delivered. Beahon was to become their very own child now, and by all accounts and indications, he was a good child and was living with them on the coastline near the river. The one with a beautiful walkway tile, if you're to believe her. Yes, that child? She's always lying...(down), but he was very well-mannered and well-behaved. But somehow, he seemed afraid, never seemed too settled with me in those days, and I? I couldn't quite see or understand, like, why, why not me. He was always somewhat distant and out of place, always itching to go a-moving on, to go out and run another race in the Harbor View forum, probably again, in this case, and the other ones carrying the combs in.

"On the tool trays?"

"Yes, say amen."

"Amen." "Nice," no matter where he would have happened to be at any given time. He seemed uneasy and was always whining. Even after finding out about it, or more like: having it registered into his skull that he was adopted, and what that meant about such kids. He never bothered to show any interest in wanting to find out more about his... like, his real birth parents. Not like other children in those days, and those parts were prone to be doing and did near the rear ends, one shoe in. This revelation of him being an adopted, childish kid happened at the age of thirteen. (Supposedly so). Well, that would have been by the official birth records, as it was to show back home in the yard to hurt him, but you know. He was a brilliant kid, and very artistic too, even before he turned twelve, per you, and your stories. His fame as the "go-to guy" in the body art community and the world at large, inasmuch as it pertained to body art and clinical massage, was well established by then that he was "The man." He was well-traveled, too. Wherever the big events were being held, BDV was sure to be there in attendance and catering to you, on the shelf. If not on the bed by himself, and you? One such event was coming up soon. It was high on the radar for the next few months, on the full moon. In another life, though, BDV was probably known as someone else, by many other names. "Oh?" "Yes, Bro," he may have existed in other dimensions too, as it would appear to some of them on the plane by admission, and you? He would have managed to carry over incremental residues of his past existences with him into the human body. The one he now lugs around heavily on the go, to somebody. He was still weighed down by the limitations of it, as things were beginning to show. Sit, sit. Sit on it, yes. Like so. Limitations such as those that are common to all humans. But not all of those would apply to this new man, not him, no. Not all of those limitations, it would have seemed. He needs to be innovative and adaptive, though, to begin to adjust to the here and now, no? “Yes,” as much as may be “humanly” possible. Go.

Chapter 20: Tattoo Hack Job

Angela was rather cranky the morning after. Her whole body ached like sour pudding on the saucer. The freshly tattooed site there at the back of her neck was raw and oozing bloody discharge. It had never hurt that much before. But now it’s hitting her hard behind the gated door chord near the yard. “Oh lord! Not again.” She was a long way from the “total coverage” she wanted in her quest to become “Total” by the time she’d turned twenty-one. But she was well on the way there and hurrying on. Her pain tolerance levels up until then were, without question, dope. The way the latest hack has been acting up on her lately, though, makes her (for the first time in her life) want to question some things; to lose hope and go about hanging on to the known faith of Fate outrightly, no, don’t cringe, nor spite me. She was a sweet girl, a very sweet girl indeed. Despite the unkempt indigo-blue-one-day, pink the next, ready-to-change-color-in-a-wink hairdos, and the double-studded pierced tongue, more or less like yours, no? “Yes.” “I know, now go and sit down.” Her heart was as pure as gold, not in terms of the texture of the metal, though. Whereas gold is hard and cold, Angela is tender, gentle, and warm. Angie had sworn to Beahon that she would lay down her very life for him. As for him, he was in a way counting on it. He was counting on that because it was a broad and large offer. Beahon, for his part, had likewise pledged to Angie to love and never leave her ever. “Not even to the end of never, nor to the end of the ages,” clever but... He was heard saying this to her in our hearing, as it occurred. That, too, was something he was counting on more than one could have ever imagined, and for many more reasons than one overripe orange. Much more than she would ever have come to know, as much as it was to be aligned with his plans to make and use her as the storage vault for his precious

Genode pellets, the cargo. Maybe even one or two other things along the way, to get wedged in between it, or welded on the car to go. He had a plan. In the meantime, though, it's business as usual for the master tattoo artist; he's got work to do, and money to make, to secure the car keys and sirloin steak. If nothing else. Beahon was by then well onto the trails of his long-lost Genode pellets. He had even retrieved a few of them already and did not want to lose track of them again to anybody. He needed to come up with a plan first, as to how and where to store them. He found such a place, very close to Angela's face, near the doorways. The plan was then set in motion, and he was well on the way to his set goals with these plans. Angela was to become his safe-keeping storage vault for the hiding of his precious kingdom things of the high-end sort. To her, he was perfect to a fault. Her knight in shining armor. Her dream lover, her everything, or something else, another. But as for him? To him, she was something quite different, something to spin; something he could never put into words, he meant. Kissing! Of course, he loved her as much as she loved him, and maybe even more so. But then, BDV "the whiz kid" was a man on a mission, and ever on the go. A mission that he could not tell or show. He could not talk about it with any mortals, no. Not with anyone. Even if he should manage to find somebody whom he could trust enough to tell his tale. Who would ever believe such a wacky old story? Oh hell! Look.

Angie's neck art has been healing quite well of late, thanks to the top-notch care she has been receiving from the master himself, to date. But he had better be good at it; the care and treatment of the wound, if nothing else to fit, in my room. Since it was his doing in the first place, the bloody mess. The apparent "kwaky" job, which was the very thing that brought about this messy situation: this whole tattoo hack job. Yes, in the first place. What Angie didn't know then, though, was that this acting up of the job wasn't a fluke at all, like something to show off at the office ball to Bob or his brother Paul. She wasn't having an allergic reaction to certain aspects of the job, as everyone around her had thought. "Why now?" She'd asked. "Why?" All the other tattoos she'd done before were the works of her beloved boyfriend and the world's most sought-after tattoo artist, and even more than that, this. They had all come out perfectly well, no problem at all to fix and go tell. However, this wasn't any regular old run-of-the-mill tattoo job gone bad. No, not on your life at all, Bob mi bredda. Okay, just nod and say, "whatev-ver." Beahon was up to something else. It was, in fact, his fault. But as for Angie, she was in some ways just like me. She was not in the least bit aware of his extra-curricular, extra-judicial endeavors around these belted asphalts in the indies on the interior. He hasn't been up until then, level with her. Although it was killing him softly inside, as it occurred, the deceit, the underhanded methods he'd used to do it. The way he had misused her trust, he dared not make her, nor us, nor anyone else, for that matter, on the bus. He dared not make anyone any wiser about what he was doing, or who he was going to be stewing. What he was after, or even what the future may hold for him and her. For all of them, later on down the shore, even. The list of treks that he took in his capacity as the master body-arts person and the go-to guy for all things: hip, cool, authentic, and legit in the world of tattoo arts and body piercings in that nook, on the nick, was growing massively. He has been traveling far and wide in recent times, too. His resume has grown more impressive with each passing day, riding right by you. On buses and highways zooming on through, on the freeway. Although the world was, at the time, seeking a sage and inviting him to come to them. He was going throughout the world seeking and searching for something else. Something quite different and unique from friends, more for himself than for them, so to speak. He was going to all those far-flung places in search of his precious lost Genodes of the week. Trying to find and return them home and off the roads in his pockets. A question for him and them to ponder then, if and when he does manage to find them. The question to consider was: what will be next on the agenda for him to do from then on, and at home? What's next for the wandering, universe-trotting, eternity, and time-hopping tattoo artist? He who had happened to fall head-over-heels in love with a starfish, no, not that, but this, I meant to say, an earthling. A member of the humanoid kind of a girlfriend? What will be next for him, and her, Angie, the girl he had fallen hard for, on his knees? What will be next for them both? Unlike how it was with the Shadow man, who had fallen for all of seven. Beahon was unlucky, it would have seemed. He fell for only one, Angie, the girl of his dreams. According to the information gathered by the scan of his chief Genode pellet, in combination with one other pellet piece. Which, by the way, at the time of recording these things to go tell-say. It was to be found, or not, (like not to be found at all) since it was already safely tucked away in a fabulous body art patch embedded at the back of Angie's neck. In the makeshift shrine beneath the wall (of hair). But what the heck, that was where they were at the time. He knew he was on the eve of a major breakthrough. Beahon had been picking up pings from various locations across the globe. Places where the original pellet pieces were showing up as ready and waiting to be recovered from the road. Two pellets were discovered to be together in one place. Somewhere way up there in a place with a name like "The European Alps," in this case. He would have discovered this by way of a signal from one of his scan results. He had to find ways to retrieve them, against his sulks. Other places were showing many hits too, other than the top ten chart of modern blues. One such "other place" was at the bottom of the sea. See? Okay, now, look at me, and say, "Yay." These two places were not the only places where the pellets were showing up for Beahon. Some were also showing up on the ice glaciers. Way up near the North Polish region, in this case, as it was, yeah! Up there for you. Beahon needed help, and he needed it fast. He knew just the right people to call up, though, if he dared to ask. Will he? Did he call them? Ansa mi nuh man!

The regional tattoo convention held in Portland, Oregon, was dope. The most productive one yet for the young master. What with all that hope? He was going there to meet and exchange ideas with the guardians and elders in the tattoo and piercing industry. By all accounts and indications, the elders were all flabbergasted by this one, you see. Like, the kid's Superior knowledge and skill sets. But all that was just cosmetic on the part of our whiz kid, making them sweat. What had gotten to him and got him most excited, though, all be it, known only to him at the time and on the go to complete the feat behind... "Oh!" "Yes, go." It was the massive amount of leads he had gathered there to find, on the trails of his lost pellets from Kingsland on the high ends, down the line, and through the years to you. He would have managed to discover not two, but five of the originals floating around right there amongst the guests and you. Embedded in their skin, yes, and rubbing up hard against the helmets within, as you'd guessed. That, along with a trailer load of information he would have gathered there on the lifestyle, cultures, clothes they wear, and the religious beliefs of "The Tattooed." You know. Tattooed people from all walks of life were there. They came from all over the world, like the man and his wife with the little girl, along with people who have been covering for several millennials, on down through the ages, to the current generation. They were (for the most part) all there. All of that was to have him excited and set to go off on a mission into the farthest, deepest corners of the globe. On the trails of the "Tattooed" from as far back as it would take him, down the road. Somewhere in the deep recesses of his mind. He knew exactly where it was going to lead him from there to go and find... something. "Let's get the ball a-rolling—babe," he'd said to her, yes, to Angie as it occurred, while leaning in to whisper it into her ear, I'd guessed before I heard. "Let's get moving, come on, let's get out of here," said Beahon to his woman there, "The game is now on." Signals had been coming in from every corner of the globe in those times, calling on him to go out there and spy in. Finding the original pellets in those conditions means taking treks into as many of those regions as possible, and eyeing them. Going off into places such as Asia, Europe, the Americas, Australia, and Africa, among other such places, was the idea, but this one is...

Chapter 21: The Meet-up

For him to concentrate his efforts on the job at hand. Beahon must first come up with a unique plan to get together with as many tattooed people and tattoo artists from throughout the world in one place as possible. He must do so as quickly as he possibly can. Off the drawing boards came these two grand ideas: a competition and a convention. "Problem solved, right?" "Yes, no mention." Well, not really, not quite yet, Neily, my friend's son. There will still be more work to be done before we get to that point, and the sweat on the seats, down home. "Really?" "You bet." So, off they went, outing the joint. There was to be one planning meeting after another, which was to see Beahon and Angie traveling together, going to far-flung places in and around the coast of Arcadia. Since he was tugging Angie along with him all the time, as his new behavior. Well, most of the time. They'd managed to see quite a bit of the world that summer because of it. But then there was the other time when... yes, hiss. Once upon one of those times, Beahon was busily traveling all over the humanoid world. Mapping out the locations where the Genodes were showing up and tracking them down hand in hand with his girl. At the same time, linking up with the elders and vanguards of the tattoo art form along the way. He made a detour on one of those treks I was to have heard tales of... That's when and where he was said to have met up with another agent. Yeah, the same one. Very conveniently, Angie was not with him on that occasion to see. She'd returned home to see about and care for her grandmother, who was reported at the time to be "not well" or something another. As such, things were reported to have been happening across the border. She was reported to be very ill. Whether or not Beahon had anything to do with it is still up for the bait they had to debate on the bottle of the pill but the fact is, they were for the first time in a long time, they were, yes, quite apart. And it would have been because of the detour. The detour he took was to meet with the agent who had been sending him messages for quite a while. They were supposed to meet up to discuss the kingdom's business and work on the kingdom's files. This was the best opportunity Beahon was presented with to get it all over and be done with quickly and be gone, to his place again, but not to sit with me. But back to Angie, his girlfriend, and to continue doing it, to them. Inside the cone patch embedded in his wrist and under the skin, the agent had been carrying a couple of messages from the kingdom with him. Which were to be delivered to the working agents, like Beahon's care and safe-keeping. Or to any of them who would have been on hand to receive them. But as it was to go, one such agent at the time was none other than Beahon, as you already know the man. At the time, too, he was just about preparing to return home to Cekkoland, true. Though unbeknownst to Angie, or any of them in the indies. Surely not you, nor me. So, they met in one of their favorite places: in the wilderness, as the case was. Deep, deep within, where the humanoid kind has hardly ever been, nor would they even venture to go easily. But as for them both, they had no trouble getting there for the meet-up. The evidence was to show this... shut up, yes, on the boat. Like, a showboat it was or some other such high-end goat. This other Cekko agent wasn't too shabby in his art after all, as it turned out; he wasn't too meager. He had to perform a skin graft on him, you know. After Beahon was done with the same type of operation to remove the cone from under his skin where it was implanted for transportation in, though. But then, it would have to be re-implanted onto Beahon's person, which he did. Not only that, but he also had some other special cargo he needed to have transported back home for the eyes of the king on the home run. So he was told, and maybe a couple of his most trusted members of the inner circle, and the household. Earlier on, much earlier on. The agent would have caught up with another rogue agent. As it was told to him at the Woodlands Days Inn. Smokey's most secretive private agent. He had happened to perform some magic of his own there at that time, on him. Had to get some things fixed, using the Kingsley bits from his Cekkoland journey kits. As far as fixing things on the earthling side of the divide would have allowed. The fix was done, oh lord! The rest must be done in Cekkoland near the throne, of this we're now prone to be proud. So, come on. Lead the caravan, homeward bound. "Oh, Lord!" Beahon's new and additional mission from then on was to get the special cargo back home to the king. Back to King Liam from his exiled agent, to him. As far as it applies to them and to what they were able to do over on the earthling side of the divide? Mission accomplished, I would never have lied. Beahon can, therefore, return to the task at hand, once more. His task was to find the lost Genodes to get them home and off the roads. As for this secret kingdom agent, though? No. But he was to be heard there humming along like so, sometimes. Back now to it, the quest to go find it. The competition was designed to search for the best talents and their best work and to bring them together in one place, of course. To acknowledge them and reward both the artists and the tattooed people with special prizes, in this case. According to the official plans. But then again, there was another one. "Like what, plan?"

"Yes." It was a gathering of all and for all. From the very least to the greatest of all of the earth's tattoo people coming in to call. Not just those who were to be vying for prizes, no, not at all. But everybody was invited to go. No surprise, Sis. It was a happy time for most; a celebratory atmosphere was in the house. They were beginning to get into the meat of the matter when it happened, over there. Just like a cry in the midnight hour, they were to hear it and go out eying the stare. Everything changed from there for them. They were in the middle of the convention when... Lots of bickering and jockeying for positions were going on. Beahon would have been adamant that he wanted certain aspects of the screening to be done privately. The elders, though, for the most part, wanted none of that. They wanted it to be "open, and real-time," as democratic a choice as possible from the start, as they could find. The atmosphere would have degenerated to the point where several minor squabbles and fistfights were happening at the venue, and then came you. Some would have been threatening to quit the whole event and head home, back to the harbor view, near the forum. At one point, some rather large and scary-looking dudes were standing in the doorways. Blocking the entrance and preventing anyone from entering or leaving to go and join up with the stowaways. All because of the squabbling of the evening. Meanwhile, several people had to be busy themselves breaking up fights and separating tassels on the floor. All around those parts, there was a boisterous uproar. So very loud and unruly was the rowdy bunch that they quickly quit their lunch. It would have taken several minutes for them to have taken notice and realized that something else was going on, outside in the park. There was another show going on in the nearby arena, of sorts. One could have almost watched it as the decibel dial tumbled one notch at a time. Someone had come running in from the outside and crying, no, not crying but shouting like you would when lying, no? "No." He was reporting, though. "Look," he said. "Something is happening out there." Look, "look up there, look..." They were shouting and pointing their fingers and noses skyward, at the incoming things and the floaters floating, it was floating in like a byword, on them. "Look up there." They were heard saying these things over the noise out the rear. Just as the silence was streaming in from the doorway and into the place where the gathering was, there on the inside. Even so, in a similar manner. The attendees were streaming out in the opposite direction, but with heads tilted up and into the sky at what they thought was about to make them all go down like a goner. While looking at the spectacle taking shape overhead. The fly-by, and in the open spaces, too, oh my! Even trying to see through the icy roof of the igloo, some of them were, even you, no? Okay then, I'll go. In a short while, short, yes, but not according to the humanoid style. Almost every last one of them was lying dead on the ice. Those who weren't trampled by the way of the stampede that followed would have been taken out of their misery by the ever-caring fighting feuders. Nice. What a sweet soothing surprise. But as for Beahon and Angie? They were the untouchables there on the ice, it would have seemed to you and me. Nice, eh, nothing even came close to either of them by way of harm, not in your dreams to see the alarm. It was as if they were boxed in some sort of invisible cage or something out of the norm. Just as quickly as it had started for the rest of them, it was all but done. Gone were they to the graveyards, almost everyone. But not for Angie and Beahon. As far as they were concerned, they had to endure the whole spectacle from start to finish, which would have lasted for days, and then some more in its... But then again, when it was all over and done. Still standing there on the floating ice continents that had been born mere moments earlier out of one. You know! Born out of the blast from the zip, pity zapping zigzag lightning balls thrown by the smoky sword-wielding girls, to fix the rest of them from the outside of their worlds. Beahon got Angie to turn around and focus more on the exhibition, then came this one. Look. After the battle, the girls, known to him as the king's daughters from the other worlds, were... "Look!" There they are, floating away atop the billowing columns of smoke like stars. With their sword raised in triumphant salute, as they turned around to look at "Har," looking at the rest of them and her. Look. They're looking back at the two standing on the ice and waving back at them. Nope, no word has been spoken to them yet. Meanwhile, Beahon waited for quite a long while. Perhaps much longer than he should have, he waited. Gazing up at the departing feminine warriors, yes, he did. Wanting to extend the moment for him, her, and the kids, perhaps. To pocket more "Crazy tales" to tell them about this and that. About what had occurred, you know, probably so, sis. Or was he doing it to delay the inevitable? Maybe. He knew what he had to do next, though, and the moment was right for it to be, so go on and text... me. There they go, taking treks, see? After trying to explain his next move to Angie, in a language she could understand and speak here in the Indies. In humanoid language, that is, the one that they both speak and understand things on this side of the divide, where he now sojourns and lives. He's doing it. And he's doing it in the hopes that she will trust him fully and not be afraid of you in it, or ask too many questions of him, while over on the other side, even. Yes. That's when he did it.

Note from the author. Thank you for choosing to read my book and for sticking with the story thus far. You must have liked it a lot. At this point, I want to ask you, my reader. Take a minute or two to post a book review on the Sales page, such as Amazon, and any other such sales page. This small gesture is so very much appreciated. And don't keep it to yourself, be sure to share this. Thank you.

Chapter 22: The Aftermath

When all was said and done, only five able-bodied people remained on the one. Well, let's say five living beings, to be on the safe side of the lords' rings; in keeping with these strange schemes of things, as they were to be heard hopping into our hearing aids. Then there were those wounded and dying there on the ice, like those, look at them, those peeping toms over there eavesdropping and looking on through their eye skins, in fear. Other than those? The five able-bodied beings would have been all those who remained standing there on the ice: the three "guarding daughters of the king." Standing on a large mound of an ice-berg the size of him, yes, the same one who was dancing with you in Australia that night, with spins, too. Beahon and Angie, on the other ice-continent, floating side by side. The companies were on the icy, cold surface... of the water, that is, the negotiations were to come in next. To Angela's utter amazement, Beahon (seemingly) has got himself a new arrangement, communicating fluidly in another language from another realm; he began communicating with the girls in a language barely even audible to her ears and theirs. "I knew it, I knew it," she thought. But as for her and her thoughts. Unlike how the talks were with him and his rattling kinds of chats, communicating with them on the ride-off. Her thoughts were in the humanoid language, as known to both of them, if not anyone else in the indies, on the high end of our rocks. "I know," she said. "I should have tugged my puppy dog along with me. He has hearing in his ears that can contain this, I'm sure." So, come and see. In the meantime. They continued arguing in their "other-dimensional languages." Just beyond the scope of her proper hearing and comprehension ranges, so it would have seemed. Despite the effort and gestures among them as they exchanged words back and forth. Which seemed to her to be similar to a loud, heated conversation going on between people in the humanoid realms. Angie just stood there spellbound, watching them. When she turned around and walked away as she was about to go home, BDV grabbed her by the arm and reverted to speaking to her in a very familiar human tongue of the day. "Wait, Angie, wait," he said, "don't leave, please."

"Welcome back, mister, let go of my sleeve," in the same breath, she said further, "...and goodbye, too. We're not from the same world here. Not of the same language, nor people, nor world views. We've got nothing in common here, so please stay the hell away from me, will you? Go away, go!" "No, no," said Beahon, reaching for her hands again, nearer to the crooks of the elbow bend than them... "Please wait, please wait, I can explain."

"Don't touch me, don't you dare touch me," she protested as Beahon tried to reason things out with her, and you, and now, look at me.

"This is it, Angie. This is what you signed up for with me, this is what we both signed up for when we were making those vows and pledges, don't you see?"

"As I remember it, there was no mention of anything even remotely resembling this, and even if there were, I've changed my mind, alright? I still do have that right, don't I? Well. I'm exercising now! This very moment."

"We didn't know all that there was in the world to know about then, Angie," Beahon replied on this wise. "We didn't know that this day and all of the events in it, all this craziness," he said while waving his open fist across his face, like this. "We didn't know then that this day would come to our eyes... "But he lied, didn't he?" "Yes," ...but that's what a pledge is about, right? "We'd pledged to each other not to jump ship as soon as the going gets a bit tough. That's what I meant when I signed up. I thought that was what you were about, too. As for me, that was enough. I was wrong." He said this over his shoulder while turning to walk away on the other side of the pond. There they are, in a zoomed-out lens, helping us to see far, look. They're still there, going at it, negotiating. Look at them as seen from here, Beahon is still begging and pleading until... What's this? What's happening to them now? "Mi blow-wow!" They seem to have come to some consensus because they're hugging now on the drifting iceberg, as far as we can see these things from the window curtains of this rather nice car, and through these eyes of ours. And then, what is this? He's doing it. He did what he knew all along that he had to; he picked up the scalding hot lightning bolt off the ice with his bare-naked toes that he'd just slid out of the snow boots and socks. Angie's eyes were closed at the time, as she savored the embracing arms behind her back. That's when Beahon would have gone and done the unthinkable, but necessary thing he knew he must and had to do. As seen through the Cekkoland lens, he was at the time, looking through. Yeah! By the way he was looking at things, unbeknownst to you. He blew himself, as well as Angie, away with him to the great beyond. Then he had to trust the hand of fate: the same sort of fate that he knew had been somewhere in there and at work throughout those times, aiding him back through the gate. All the time, in those realms, dispensations, and distances that he had managed to survive so far. Will Fate come to the rescue this time? Or is she still out somewhere dancing at the bar and boozing on cheap wine? He wasn't sure at the time, but he was wondering. Was it something that Angie had done to him? If only for a brief moment, there before the lift-off. He was in an alien, thoughtful wonderment of some sort. Will the girls be of any help? Will they come through for him and them both? Does anyone among you know how these things will turn out? No? Well. While standing there on the ice, both were locked in a warm, consoling embrace at the time. Beahon tossed a shiny yellow David's star-shaped lightning bolt across his face, like so. Yes, the embossed rock, with smoky-bluish zigzag slanting and shortened edges pointing down and outwards to the outer peripheries of the back. The same rock the girls had thrown at him while they argued in their "alien" language exchange before taking off from among them and from those territories, slack again, mounting up on columns of fire, smoke, and steam. He tossed the object over his shoulder as he would have seen them do it. He threw it behind his back, and the inferno erupted, just like that. Sending yet more columns of fire, smoke, and steam up. Up, up, and away. Sucking up the snow, the ice, and everything else with it on the way up. Including them, Angie and

Beahon. That was the end of them both as we've come to know them on this side of the divided spoke, over the ponds. Or was it?

Meanwhile, in some faraway places down the Isles. All eyes were gazing up and looking skyward. People were to be seen there stretching their faces just like a byword. Watching the scenes. Watching the fly-by is what I mean, and more. "Oh my!" Beahon came in by way of the A-chamber. He was sent into the chamber as a young man in his prime, coming out like a newborn baby, cold and crying for his mama on some faraway shore by the raging seas. He's on the way back now, carried along by thieves. Please, be sure to say it like this only if it's securely wrapped up in a sneeze. There he goes, gone, with his lover-girl on his arm, wow. Or leaning up against someone else's arm now, since she hasn't got the strength to do anything on her own, probably. She's not even leaning onto warmer something, things like...like... No, not even that one tooth's jawbone near those bike... bike, bikes of theirs. And then, there might yet be more comers to come hanging around us on these earth stones. We're all waiting to see who that will turn out to be, or what will be happening next, to you and me.

Chapter 23: Stolen Away to Summary Land

The little incident on the ice would have gotten out of hand very quickly indeed. The whiz kid wanted to have certain people segregated and set apart by themselves for purposes known only to himself in the waste in deeds, yes, indeed, seemingly. He led the charge in formulating the rules. Many elders did not like that at all, and were quick to point it out to him, over the point of the tools, even. Making it clear to him that although he might be seen by some of them there as the most popular person amongst them, this time around. It was, in fact, they, the elders, who had been there all the while holding down the forts, keeping things together for ages, and grounding the corks. He was out of order for wanting to come on in and steamroll over them like a bulldozer of sorts. "Furthermore," they reminded him, in somewhat of a threatening sort of way that he should not forget that he was still just a kid and should give them the "bleeding" respect that they had rightfully earned. The younger ones amongst them, though, were (seemingly) on the... "Go." No, not that, but on the kid's side, ready and willing to stand up and fight to defend him, not me, I'm bright. And then all hell would have broken loose, but such was not to be found coming only from among those groups. In no time, some fires were blazing on the ice up there. Glacier cracking and falling like rice to dish out and share. Ice melting, waters rising, temperatures rising. All that could be raised high was rising. And the fallers, yes, they too, were active, as they were to be found falling on you, and more, much more than these. BDV could not come all the way out and tell them what he was really up to. It would have been better for them, though, if they had relented and allowed him some slack all the way through. At least it would have been better for those he was there trying to screen out of the running. That is because he really wanted to save them from themselves and from drowning. If they had planned on living and surviving beyond that point. That would have been the thing to do without denying him his bargaining point anymore. But then. It was not long afterward that those girls, his friends. The supposed daughters of the king were to have shown up at the conference center, and they were not alone. Nor were they out there to play the trombone. They weren't playing anything. No, not on this day's win, so they were showing up there with their smoking swords, wielding them at them and cutting through the flesh and bones of the soon-to-be corpse. The flesh and bones of man and beast, ice and glacier alike, like a hot knife through butter at night. Meanwhile, smoke, fire, and steam were billowing upwards to darken the elements above them, higher, and what could a generation of the very overly tattooed do to solve them, liar? Nothing at all, nothing it would seem. They were not prepared for anything quite like that, not in their dreams, nor anything even remotely resembling it. So, how were they supposed to react? How could they even have known that, and these other things? They had never seen anything quite like that before in their lives, massive flying objects, or creatures as they really were. There was one company, then two, as seen by a few of them, and then by many more, even you, no?

"No."

"You mean to tell me, you didn't see those feuding two?"

"No."

"Oh, well then, I think I'd better go and spend some money on the children." Because... Yes, as for the rest of us and them, we saw it all, just like I was saying, they all saw it. The rest of them. They all saw the beasts within their riding frames, way up there in the skies, on a collision course above the earth on high. "What is this?" He, the chief and elder, had asked rhetorically, while staring up at the seemingly tiny object approaching from the north side of the oval-shaped sky for them to see. The same sky that was hanging there and watching the floaters-guys passing by me. As if he wanted to come in and spread the blanket over and across the camp and the entire region around the square to frighten me. The thing is, it was getting bigger in the eyes of the people-figures on the approach, and then. From the corner of his eyes, he caught a glimpse of something else, in surprise. The other one was coming in, as if to sit on the shelf, then out of the South end, there appeared other objects, heading in the opposite direction, yes. Both seemed set on a collision course, but of course. Abruptly, he sat up. "What, the hell, is this?" Again, he wondered out loud, in a querying speech. The whole company would have exited the door of the massive igloo by then and gone outside to explore. Heads tilted backward as they gazed at it, yet some more, mesmerized by the wonders taking shape in the open skies over their heads. One by one, the group gathered around the leaders and elders to pick their brains. None of them being sure, it would seem, whether this was an actionable event and whether or not they should be getting into action mode and preparing to fight for the win. Not getting any command from the leaders as to what to do, they stood their ground and watched, just like you. Yes, every last one of them, and you did nothing but that. By the time they would have managed to get themselves caught up with their senses and started scampering about for their lives. The feature show was well underway in the air and the skies. Overhead, the two armies were getting closer. One was waving a banner, in the morning sunshine, yellow. The other was sporting indigo blue. One company rode on reptile and bird-like creatures. The other one rode on zebra-striped beasts like you, and on some horse-like creatures, too, not a few. The battlefield was an open space in the elements above the Earth. The conference attendees, every last one of them, like these. Tattooed people. Tattoo artists and elders. As well as Angie and Beahon, there, elbow to elbow, bare. They were all spectators at this point. Apparently, melted-bowelled, scared-out-of-their-wits spectators for the most part. Mostly shaking like jelly in their snow boots of sorts. Sparks were flying overhead like fireflies in the night. Smoke swished around the camps of the feuding two as swords ricocheted off the tough, brasslike outer coats of the reptiles and the other flying beasts. The occasional strike was getting through to hit hard upon the flesh so sweet. Sweet sliced and diced beastly flesh, yes, like meat. Blood was oozing out and falling to mix in with the icy cold water by the boisterous waves of the roaring sea below them. Now, look at these and tell me if you know any of them, and then. Go on, strike one up for carelessness on the part of Cespedoran and his clan's massive lead reptile, as we have come to know his friends. It so happened that. The horse-like beast would have found the soft underside of its neck between the anxious jaws of one of those zebra-striped beasts. The beast clamped down with a king-sized pit-bullion bite and would not let go, no. Not for all the water in the ocean beneath them, you know. The reptile moaned and groaned as the combined reptilian train, plus one clinging zebra-striped beast without a known name, was swirling around in a funnel-like shape, pointing downward and into the ocean for an escape. They pierced the surface of the water. Plunging through and disappearing for a while before rising to shoot back up and out of the water again a few moments later. With a mighty burst of speed and agility. While spinning around in a dizzying whirlwind like her, look, listen. Listen, listen to them, can you not hear them? "Yes." "I see." That is the roaring sound of the people's screaming, along with the howling of the raging beasts all evening. But the struggle continued. Look, the fighting beasts are swerving around. Twisting the night away and spinning around in circles still. Then falling through the water's surface and down into the deep again, if you will. Up and down, up and down again. It went on like that for what might have amounted to several weeks in human time measurements. Months, perhaps. But this was not a dream of your baby and his pops, nor was it happening in another faraway realm, I mean. In a distant time zone and space far away from him and them, as in dreams. It was happening right there before their eyes, yes, in your face, guys. Beahon was among them as an Earthling living with them. He wasn't even thinking of himself as anything, nor being anywhere near what or who he was of old. The person or the agent from the king's household. On this day. He was known to them there and was trying hard to convince himself that he was, in fact, just that, like, okay, and fair. Just there among them as Beahon. Or BDV, the tattoo whiz-kid, as was the norm. Of course, other than for Beahon himself, (who is now hoarse), none of them knew anything about any of this. They didn't know who those entities were, either, or what they were bickering about on the frozen river. All the conference attendees who were just about to have a showdown of their own on the ice mere moments earlier were to be consumed in the melee. But somewhere in his mind. The earthly Beahon could not help but think he had seen that type of thing somewhere before. Anyway, as for him, and how he happens to see some things now, like mean and lean. "Life is a continuous journey," he said to nobody in particular, Leigh. "We discover and learn as we go along." How long will all these things last? It all depends on the luck of the draw, one might suppose in class. He forgot more, though, much more than most people will ever come to know. Or could even have learned in an entire humanoid lifetime down here below. "Things get a bit fuzzy sometimes," he said, memories tend to fade, too. Just like the anchor tattoo there on his wrist was to do. Again, after those things. The folks there would have looked out across the waters and seen it again; the loopy dopy, wobbling, floating thing. Riding the waves while leaving to go away and deceive them. Occasionally, it raises its head above the water and then dives back down. As seen more than once before, by many people back home over there. Or even just a few, sometimes. The Shadow Man, even, his kind, and others like them, and you ain't lying. By many others, too, even earthlings. Some like those assumed this beast was somehow linked to Cespedoran, the vile one, and his clan. Lost and languishing out there in the deep, as the story goes, yes, that one. Out of the comfort of his long-established, but even just as long-lost to him, home of abode. His habitation, though, is back over there in Cekkoland down the road. But according to the unofficial story, as was told to me by... by somebody, Cespedoran, the vile one had grabbed the Genode pellets and run with the king's guards in hot pursuit of him. Along with some leather-clad women riding on zebra-striped beasts, and chasing after to capture and rope him back in. Or to get him to come back and partake of the feast on the home end, perhaps it was for that, like, reason. But they could not because he was much too fast and therefore got them lost easily. He's now languishing somewhere out in the stratosphere and wondering if he will find redemption again at the pleasure of the king. Shad was mishandled and trusted with the recovery role. Similarly, he was again taken out of the fold to be made a goner. But his work is not yet done, even though he's still number one and is back home again and living with him in the kingdom. This serpentine creature seems to be living somewhere in the deep, dark parts of the ocean. It has a huge, elongated head, figured out of all other bodily proportions. With a strong-looking jawbone and sharp-looking teeth. A pair of ill-figured wings, too, with which it grabs what it wants to bite and eat. Wings shaped more or less like a badly designed umbrella, and you. On which it would often try to mount up out of the water and go after that fella, yeah, that's who. But its long, wobbly tail keeps on dragging it back down. So, into the water, it would stay or go. After sinking under the water, rising, and doing the roundabouts again for long periods before disappearing for even longer periods, like, as if hiding. Only to reappear at other times, other dispensations, or even in some other regions of the world, doing the same sea-serpentine type of dance without his girl, yet again. He's probably out there searching for her, even now, well, whispering this in my ear, he waved his hand across his face and said, "What — ev — ver." Mi blow-wow. For several days on end, the fire would have burned. There was a fire on the ice in the Austrian Alps, as the event would have turned out. Not long afterward, there was an earthquake. A massive earth tremor had shaken the South Pacific region and diverse places in North America. Then came a tsunami and a flood in Alberta. The water never receded from some of those flooded areas. The ice glaciers never returned to their natural states either. At that first glance. It didn't seem to have had much effect on the environment or the local temperature in the future, but over the long run, the effect was unmistakable. It's the same way as how things are likely to go sometimes with the wrong rum and steak edible. Warmer weather was being reported across the globe, and increasingly so was the node. While some earthlings were seeing these new developments as a good thing. Good for business, for crop production, and such things, so they say. Yet many would have been there sounding the alarm anyway. What was to follow next was major floodwaters, more shattering earthquakes, like, let's say, yours off your daughter's tirade, okay? More tsunamis and radical weather shifts. Beahon and Angie were taken away; they're gone now, transported over onto another sphere, but...

Chapter 24: While Others Were Sleeping

While Liam was slumbering there that night. Shadow Needleman sneaked out of the Palace and out of the white light, using the extra skill that he'd garnered over on the earthling side, but — "What about...?" "Yes, I know, I know about him, that smoking Smokey thing." While he was dragging his feet around. The weight of Cekko's life now weighs him down. Someone would have hopped right onto his regular stamping ground and wreaked havoc on everything for him, as was known. Yes, on everything, Smokey, that clown. "He's so spooky, but — "Sit down, we're not quite yet done." Blinded by fear, anger, and suspicion.

Smokey let his guard fall hard under his hand again. He, too, was fast asleep, my friends. Been working for too long, and worrying his brain over his feet, in the wrong. He was wearing his blinking eyelids down, too. Troubled over not having the reports coming through. Coming in from his toady agent son while running home and bumping into you, no? "No, that's not true." "Well, if you say so, Boo, what the hell! What can I do, other than to go on and tell...?" So here we go again, trying to tell this story to you and him, same as he had often done, to friends, to spin. Did his special-agent son abandon him? He was left alone there and wondering. But as for Shadow, he had been looking on and taking notice of those and such things, or the others. He would have noticed and seen by way of the passing scenes that Smokey was losing sleep, and for sure, he could not continue to go on like that. Not for much longer than the time to last the week, running on flat, behind the brewery door, secured under keys and Cekkolandee locks. It was for sure, the place where Shad had happened to see the secret door, and he also knew the score. He knew that this time, Smokey would be sleeping through, for days, weeks, even. Just like he was known sometimes to be doing with Steven, and you. "And tonight?" Tonight, Liam has a heavy load on his mind. So he's resting a lot more of late than is the norm; he's stretching out to sleep again, under the dim rainbow-lit shrine. Not snoring this time, which is a sign, but... Shadow doesn't mind. He's grown accustomed to how things are around this neck. Tonight he has got important matters to tend to, so what the heck, look! Down in the dungeon, the Shadow man went. Snaking his way around ropey webbed corners and the many mazes of bends. And then, look at him, he's there. With the master key in his hand for the pocket where the lock on the handle was to be found, to release the staircase up from the underground. Now he's climbing, slowly and carefully, to avoid running the risk of alerting somebody. The darn thing is old and very rusty. The squeaking sound could wake up one of his buddies. Can't risk that, shouldn't be moving too fast. But finally, he's here at last. He had managed to make it out and up to the attic. It should be easier to get back down to Smokey's office. From there, we'll come back here. "Where?" "Here." Look at it, that's his leather seat. Now, swear on the spit that you won't snitch, because this is it, the real "it." As it is, he's there. From here, he'll be in the clear, seeing more clearly the way to go, while going to see about his current business, there. No? So now he's in Smokey's domain and fiddling around. Studying architecture and the beauty of the town. From up there, look, the street lights are shining down on him and them. But the charts, and all the ways and means that aid him in the wonder-working things, of that same Smokey, now simmering in dreams, allowing strangers to invade the Inn. It was there that they were to be found; they were all to be found there. Filed away and tied together, bound up, in Smokey's office spheres, now, continue to focus, man. There he is now, just like a mouse, the Shadow man. Searching through the house, trinket box in hand. Hopping around on his softly padded heels this time, from the deep basement storage space to the high office, on the upstairs, climb. All of these are accustomed to bouncing Smokey's knees on his heels behind. But this time, it's a stranger who is there, rampaging through the dusty tears and wares. Rubbing things up against the out-of-service dusty shrine. Pulling out drawers and chairs that weren't his or mine, he was not even denying the sitting behind. Cupboard doors swung wide open and then closed shut again. The filing cabinet was not to be spared, and look! Hot items were to be found coming mostly out of there, and them. And the book. That's the hook; that was how and where he found the fix for the problem of today's tiny bits, for fish hooks. The Genode pellet fixer, too, was there among all of that, and this, and you? But his troubles weren't over yet, as was his luck. He also had to find ways to get it out of there to do its work. "Yuck." With the rest coming in pairs out of the office spheres and popping out of the hands of the next agent to come. Beahon, as it would have turned out to be him, yes, that man. "Because...?" He was one of them and was soon to be coming in, riding in on the wings of the wind. Coming home with the darn thing to give it to him. He also had to work overtime to get the cargo to change hands over there in Cekkoland among the shrines, soon.

As it turned out, Shad had a plan. As if you couldn't on your own figure out that one. He had to set up a unique situation where Beahon could get the cargo out from under his hands and then pass it on. Or tuck it away where no other man but his Cekkolandee brother, that very same Shadow man, the other, would be able to find it. And then go get the eyes and effort of King Liam behind it. For sure, he did. The Shadow Man did. He found such a place and made it safe on the hide where it was hidden. Yes, it was him. The Shadow man, not the King, oh come on, in. It was he who was to get the entire job done properly, too, in the end, not you, and make good on his escape from all of them. "True." So, when those faraway people were looking skyward, and would have seen the fly-by vehicle as it passed overhead, way up high like a weevil to the bye road, yes, as already said. He was there, too. Beahon and Angie were there riding with the girls on the zebra-striped beasts through, oh my. But how did they get there? Don't lie. No, no earthling seemed to know, or even care. No watch-and-peeps. No peep show was keeping seats over there. But as for him? If there was one thing the Shadow man knew for sure, it was that Beahon was soon to be passing through that door, as one of the first places for him to pass through on his arrival back on Cekkoland's shore, in his home-bound landing shoes, as with other things more that he has got to do to complete the issue. He would have spent a little extra time working to fix the panel and the lock on the front entrance door frame. The one leading in and out of the chamber again. Yes, the assimilation chamber, as he was to remember, my friends, Beahon was game. Would have lived up to his name. He's going to be spending at least one more day on purification rituals. Same too, is Shad, but not with the gals he's had, not this time. Just on his terms, as usual, yes. As is the custom with him, he's Shad and very bad. But he needs to go in there to do some good for once. Like, to try and make good on his plans. But unbeknownst to any under Smokey's command, well, anyone but Beahon. Beahon is still his man; Smokey's, right? But he's also the Shadow's man at a different level of the plan tonight. So, they have got to get together in secret. This way, not the other, as he did. This was to enable the exchange of the toad corpse "The Crept." Plus, the other information he would have homed it back with. Now Shad is there, in the very place where he and others like Beahon have long harbored fear. In the A-chamber, you'd asked? Yes, right there. So far as he was able to remember, I guess, but look here! He went in there first, like, while Smokey still snores in slumber and curses. Lying down in his rooming chamber under the church, Sis. "Or was... wasn't it like, in his brewery workshop space?"

"Worse, Sis." Now, Shadow is there, trembling and shaking, hoping that he won't have long to wait before they come to bring the weary wanderer in. Everything is about timing, but the Shadow Man is still on his rhyming and shaking, and this is surely not his favorite place to be in... Lucky for him, though, activities are now on the go. Look, here they come. This is girl number one, Estella, the youngest of them, now in the cellar to be cleansed. She should not have long to stay in, and Shad has no business with her, just with him. Good so far, but still. "Step it up a bit more, please. "You mean, the speed?" "Yes." These hazardous conditions are surely not good for me and him, there on his knees. With the temperature constantly changing, and having him there wanting so much to but still can't sneeze echem. He's there, rolled up in a tiny pan, behind the machine in a fetal position. Can hardly breathe. Smokey, you'd better take heed. Step it up, man, the speed. Get me out of this cram, yeah, said Speed. From this tiny space where I now am." One, two, three, look, the girls are all done, now it's he, him, Beahon. He's in, but... "Why is it taking so long, Shuts! Isn't he already a Cekkonian, and wasn't he put through the proper program to get him out on the mission? Smokey, that Smokey, he's up to something spooky." Or is he? Oh sheet! No. "What the hell is this? Oh! Look." Smoking Smokey just tumbled over and fell—buff. Oh man, look at that one. Shad can surely use a little bit of luck on his arms. Up, up, up, and fast. Get moving along, at last. Let's get it on, man, no more snoozing around. Let's get this done. Go, get the move on him, yes, now, run. Now! Look at him. Shad is at the front door of the chamber and hastening to get out of the inner door, as I remember, I can't be too sure. He's pulling Beahon out and getting into the task in another tiny chamber to go perform his work, removing the cargo from his skin and then quickly tucking him back into the cork within… Before Smokey gets to his waking point again, to get in there and look after his friend, Beahon. But now, he's got to go sit back down and wait for Smokey to come back and open up the gate and get him out of that scorching place. But wait, yes, wait, he must, enduring the heat and inhaling dust. Smokey is back now, good for him, but not for us, nor them. Getting Beahon out is the first thing for him, and to stop the fuss, the next game. But then, he never knew what'd hit him, again. That Smokey frame. The blinding lights and powdery dust came at him from behind the door at us. No, not really at us, but him, just him, tough luck, but great sling. Out the door of the chamber, the A-chamber, as he was to remember. That's where it came from to hit him, that Smokey un-sober thing. It hit him down to the floor again, and he couldn't seem to remember his name. So now Shad has got hold of the key to get himself out of the brewery. He's out now and running away, through the streets in the light of day. They are looking at him and wondering. Who in the health scare is he, and why is he running so fast away from me? But, that's the Shadow man's luck, his business, and his only. On his way home to go and get homely. He's got it.

"Yeah! I know. Got the rabbit in his pocket, no?"

"No, it's not a rabbit. It's the toady toad corpse of it, and the other bits from Beahon's journey kit." But then, oh, "she-at I it." In the end, or more like, nearer my lord to the end of some of them over there and then. Like, even that Smoking Smokey friend. "And why is that?" You'd asked? It's because he's the problem. For instance, just for instance, my friends. Shad was to be allowed to do the honor of the toad reveal to Smokey, yes, him, again. On the heels of his going away to go shack up with them, or something. Other than that, he was just sitting there, relaxed — "On a rock, right?"

"No, he's long done with that, yuh too bright." I mean, you. But, on the king's right hand, or the left. Whichever one was to suit him better, or on either of them, best. Well, while in the public's eyes to see, I guess, and constantly so around that neck. But you didn't hear it from me, no? "You bet," and that was to become the norm around the Cekko palace and throne, in those recent times, as it was to be known. Now watch the shadow man at work, again, in his supposed retirement lane, in Cekkoland.

Yes, word play is the order of the day around here, remember? Yeah, man, a Jamaica yaad mi come from, sorry, I meant to say, I'm Jamaican born and bred. Okay?

Chapter 25: Spoiled Rice.

Shadow Needleman is back in more familiar territories now, nice. Not wilderness territory, nor even near-wilderness territories as before. He's home, really and truly home. Home watching people as they go about, doing what they do, or do without. He's watching the scenes too, watching things as they unfold, on you. So we were told by guess who? Yes, you, a friend of the household. Beahon and Angie should be back there by now, too, being carried in through Smokey's hands while being borne along on some zebra-striped beast, back to you, perhaps. Sporting brand new Cekkolandee shoes and socks. But over here in the realms of the humanoid kind? Strange things are happening, there's no denying it, yet. Many new players are on the scene over here, you bet. Interacting with the earthlings and drinking beers, while wiping sweat and shedding tears. It was out of favor for a friend that Bauctnumboulei would have taken on Jay's daughter again as a friend, and then as a lover, although he was twice older than them. He was doing it as a favor for one of his Cekkolandee neighbors, a friend of the kingdom and the inhabitants of the highest realm, but then again. He was known to them only as "Capo — the gentleman," and captain, sometimes like, when asked of him, be kind. She was his Wonder Woman and his number one. He was zero.

But then she began to become a hero, his hero, or heroine, the same, then, together, both of them began to be number one again. Well, as for him, he was nothing, remember? Nothing more than zero. So this was to be his first shot at being number one for him, down here below. But although he was there to help out a friend. He was also there to try and get a somewhat deeper insider's view of things, of earthling things. Trying to find out all he could about how such things go in the humanoid world and realm. He had to get into the trenches and meet up with the people on the benches. "The women even?" Yes, them and you, Steven. But unlike you, he would have met quite a few while trying to find a way to climb out of the dark hole where he had been plunged. According to family lore, and you, to his history, too, and to get his lunch behind Jay's door, daily. "Like biscuits to crunch some more, eh? "Yeah, Leigh." He ought to be in a much higher place than this, but here he is, decorating Jay's business. Old soldiers like him never die. They just plan the war and send young soldiers, or younger soldiers like Jay, for instance, not me. Send them to the battlefield to suffer, to bleed, and to die. Not him, though, no. He won't die, this old soldier won't let this one die. He really likes the guy. That's one of the many reasons why. You know, that's the reason he had to bother. He's an old man and a father, having seen and done quite a bit in his "lives" and times. Yes, I know. Some of you might be found to have issues with those terms as they go, like lives and times. So, go, there's no denying it, no. But as far as this old man is concerned, he has had many, very many, many lives and times. Now, look at him and learn.

The old man is sitting in the corner and stroking his long white beard. Stroking it with his slightly shaking right hand, yeah, look! Right there. The overgrown fingernails now and then would have hitched on a strand or two, invoking more effort into the rhythmic glide of his hand over the silvery-white woolly strands, and you. In his left hand, he held a lit cigar. Across the dimly lit room, the other man, maybe 30 years or so his junior and the proprietor of the business, was busily making himself look busy with his hands like these, again, yes indeed. Jay is a hard worker and the chief cornerstone of this village, the whole region perhaps; he's well-privileged. Now and then, he would have shot the old man a menacing look as he carried on doing yet more "nothing." Theirs had become a strained one, a strained sort of relationship in recent times, and worsening, my man. Well, not really "theirs." The old man has got nothing against him, to be fair, in fact, he really liked the guy. That's the whole reason why. He liked his daughter, too, his whole family, as a matter of fact, and you? That was what had gotten him into this mess in the first place. He was looking out for his interest and for that of his friends on the ice blades of the kingdom. The whole realm, even. He was looking out for the greater good of all, for everyone. Jay is "The man" around these parts. It's he who gets things done throughout the whole region if you ask; they depend on him for anything and everything. The old man was very wise and would have seen and done a lot in his time. He was a well-decorated veteran of the thousand-year war. Or was he lying? Lost almost everything and everyone whom he would have cared about, and for, so he had said. But he struck up a deep friendship with Mister Jay at the depot, yes, mi bred. Whenever he was not at the veteran's office or service center. One would be more than likely to find him there, at the depot, even at the entrance, Sir. Sitting, chatting, smoking, and stroking. Just wasting time away joking with him. The relationship would have become strained when he was to... The captain... Yes, Captain; that's what they all called him, "Captain." Or Capo. If he had any other name(s), few would have known it. But the captain would have spoiled it. He's the one who'd spoiled the relationship. It was a rather busy day there at the depot. Jay was really busy at that time and raring to go. Not just "Acting the part" to make himself look busy and smart, as was the custom, and just showing off from the counter behind the doorstop. "No, it wasn't like that, wasn't that kind." He had just received fresh supplies and was in the middle of stacking and restacking. Jay was cleaning out the bins, tossing out the old and spoiled residues of the rice and putting the new ones in. In the proper places for them. The captain had been watching and offering to lend a hand whenever and wherever it was needed. But then he ventured out further and offered a bit more than just a hand. "Yes?" Yes, he did. He offered up some advice to the man. Wrong call again on this bid? Or was it the wrong timing? "Same vice, kid." That wasn't all that he did there, but continue, I'm in. Jay was into preparing the rice barrel, cleaning it out, and getting it ready for the new supply. The old supply was old indeed. The remaining pound or two of rice at the bottom of the barrel was dark and moldy. Surely it wasn't any longer fit for human consumption; it was even smelling somewhat foul, Leigh. So, Jay wanted to throw it out. That was when and where the captain had to step in. Couldn't silence his mouth, you know, like, from talking out. "No," he said, "you shouldn't do that, mi bred. You can't just throw your money away like that."

"What are you talking about, Capo?" He didn't bother to answer, no, not verbally anyway, to shout... Oh! The captain stepped to the barrel and took the container with the spoiled rice. He walked over to where the new supplies were. Then, proceed to toss handful after handful of spoiled rice into the bin with the new ones. "Are you out of your cotton-picking mind?" Jay lunged at him from the counter behind, like the nuance, he is. Pushing him aside, and taking the remainder of the spoiled rice out of the old man's hand, and then. Luckily for him, he would have tossed the bowl away... instead of tossing it at his head to make him pay. The old man just sat there where he had fallen, leaning his back up against the wall and looking. He's looking at Jay and stroking his silvery beard in the usual way.

Meanwhile, Jay would have been there trying his best to pick grain after grain of spoiled rice from among the good ones in the bin. While sulking and turning to cast menacing looks at the old man periodically. (Grinning). He just sat there, stroking still, and staring back at him. "I think you'd better go, just leave," he said to the old man there, shaking his head, over his sleeves. "Go please, go." And that's what he did; he got up and left. He'll be back, though, maybe tomorrow, not too sure about that part, but not many days from now, that's for sure. He's an old man now; the time cards are stacked against him in the shady players' hands somehow. Unlike the old saying that goes: you've got the watch, but we've got the time. No, the old man hasn't, he hasn't got that much time. That much he knew, so he's got to do what he has got to do; he knows it very well. And quickly, too, as you can tell, now, look at this and that. He's back there the following day, and Jay is at it again, the same way, busily making himself look busy, while casting menacing glances at the old man who is sitting there again in his usual place and doing his usual thing. Or his bundle of nothings, and stroking his beard. Smoking a cigar, and looking at him, looking at Jay. Looking back at him somewhat like this way. Jay was adamant in his resolve to say, "I will not speak to him ever again, never." Two hours later, he narrowed it down a notch. "Well, maybe sometime in the future, but surely, not today." Now watch, they're talking. Well, he's the one doing the talking, Jay is talking, or more like asking questions. Many questions, rhetorically.

"How could you? What in the name of the gods got into you? What got into you? Have you completely lost your bloody bleeding mind?" Jay ranted at him from behind the counter, while pressing a spiraling pointy finger up against the side of his head, spinning him in, Spinning away at reeling him in like a thread. He didn't respond. The captain, if he's nothing else, is a wise man. He knew enough to know that, no matter how many questions were coming at him from Jay in his current state, firing off faster than a pistol shot at this gate. No answer, none at all, would have made one iota of sense to him. No matter how logical or reasonable it might have been. So, Capo, the captain, just continued doing what he had been doing; stroking, smoking, and watching Jay, still there doing what he does, all day. "You're a big, big man around here, you know," he said, just before closing time and before leaving for bed and home, before he would have been booted out again by the fierce anger of Jay's wrath alone. They've both got a whole other night ahead of them to think about some things, in fact. But tomorrow is coming fast, and everyone knows that "Capo," the captain, will be back. Sitting there again, smoking his cigar, and stroking, and...

It's a big shopping day today. Most village folks are early in getting the shopping done. "Yay!" Capo would have seen it all, and more "some," as usual. He was always there and had his lunch there too, as usual. Haven't exchanged a word with Grumpy old Jay yet, though. But that will change soon, no? They're alone together there again. Nothing strange from the norm, my friend, only that. They have not been on speaking terms over the past couple of days, as you already know, and yet more before you go. But now? "What is to become of them? What's going to happen to them?" The old man was heard asking. Seemingly, rhetorically. But it wasn't his rambling rhetoric at all, the question was pointed squarely at Mister Grumpy, sorry, I meant to say, at Jay. At Mister Jay. Jay, though, would have just turned and cast a grudging glance at him before carrying on doing the nothing he has taken to be doing more and more of lately. "Why, why? Want to tell me why you would have done something like that? Why, why?"

"Well, welcome back, Mister G." Jay stopped in his walking away tracks and turned to face him, not me.

"G? What the hell are you talking about now?"

"G, as in 'grumpy.'" He just fanned him off with a wave of his hand and stamped... Like, while quickly walking away upon some stylish foot-play. Ugh, aah, aah, and aahing some more at him. "Lunatic," he said, softly under his beard, near his head. "What do you think would become of them if you weren't around? Yeah, I know, you seem to think that I'm crazy. Outright mad, perhaps, well, maybe. But I'm doing them all a favor here. More than you or any of them themselves even know. Or will they even care?" Jay is listening now. He's leaning across the counter on an elbow and staring at the old man sideways while thumb-scraping the sweat from his brow, in his customary way. Probably still thinking that the lunatic asylum is on one of those side days somehow, on a day off, you know! But he's nonetheless listening.

"Did you get all of it? The spoiled rice, did you get every lost grain out from among the good ones? Well, nice, my good man. Can't afford to sell spoiled rice to your very loyal customers now, can you? You've got to throw it away, right? Yeah. Go on. Throw it out, your money. Go throw it out. But you've got to make absolutely sure that your customers don't throw theirs away. Their money is good, but yours is bad, okay? So go right on, go ahead. Go on and throw yours away so that they don't have to throw theirs away. We'll see what becomes of them and their money when you're done and gone. Or even before that day, should come strolling on. We'll see what becomes of them when you're done and gone broke after throwing your money away." The old man was done, for the time being at least. He raised himself from where he was sitting there on his usual seat. Brushed his backside with sharp hand strokes back and forth like this. Sounding it off loud enough for folks to hear outside the doors and further afield. Like, far off from over there where the blue smoke comes across those hills, of theirs. He then puffed grey smoke from his cigar and walked out of there, leaving Mr. Jay there watching, as he went his way. He was sure that Jay was watching him, but he never even turned around to look back at him. He'll have a lot to think about tonight before he cozies himself down at home to watch the fight. If he's as wise a person as the old man has come to regard him as being, and bright. He'll surely have a different perspective on a few things, come tomorrow, by evening, good night. He still wasn't in a talking mood the following day and the next. He casts out quite a bit more lingering stares in the old man's way while he goes about doing his pile of nothing, though, still sulking and vexed. A full week would have passed before they were to exchange words further. Be it on that one or any other matter. But the old man has got things to say. He was aware that the time cards were still stacked against him and slipping away. He didn't have the luxury of messing around and pussy-footing around the issues. So, he would have spoken, and just like he'd thought, Jay was ready to listen, if not to act. And now, here is he, Mr. Jay, for thee. Just looking at him without interrupting, no cross-talking from him, nor butting in.

"You're a big man, Jay. You're a very important pillar of this community, yay. If you and your business were to go under, the whole community would suffer. You're too big to fail, so what do you do? You let them help you out in bearing the burden. Let them carry some of the loss for you, or all of it. Why should you bear it all and let them go free when they won't even be any better off than they are now, as it is, with you bearing it for them? Listen to me, Jay." Standing up on his feet again and facing him, he began to say, "What I did there, the spoiled rice and all, I didn't do it for you at all. I did it for them, Jay. I did it for them. Look at it this way. Most people are already in the habit of 'picking and sifting' through their rice and washing it before they cook it. It's precisely those types of things that they're searching for and removing from the batch of it. They search for such things and sift them out from amongst the good rice before cooking. So, that handful of spoiled rice that was tossed in by... by someone, well, by anyone at all. That would have weighed in at about what? Let's say, a half-pound, one pound at the most. All of that would have been coming out of your pocket. Cutting into your profit and hence, also cutting into the amount of cash that you would have left to go back out there shopping, for more of it, you know, like. For yet more products to be brought back home into the village for these very folks to be able to have the supplies that they need to eat and grub it, on the row, no? On the other hand, though. If and when you toss it in like so, in the same manner as I did it in the bin there for you. The person who comes to your place and buys a pound of rice from you, as is the case here, would have helped to bear the burden of the loss, not just you. Although the real impact on that person's bottom line would have been negligible, if at all noticeable. Each household would probably get just a few grains of the spoiled rice in the pound they had bought for the price. But they would have caught it and removed it from the final product that ended up on their table, nice, eh! Nice. This is by them doing the very thing they have always been doing, and as they are well able to do. 'Pick and wash the rice before cooking it,' in a stew. Not a problem. None at all, for them. But as for you? How do you think you got those wandering grains of untreated rice in the bag you purchased from the wholesale outlet last night? How do you think they got in there amongst the treated ones you'd gotten for the price?" Just like that, he was done and gone. The old man is long gone now; he has moved on from there, where Jay and his friends are, but wow. Mr. Jay has surely got a new perspective on a few things today. Speaking of cooking, I had to say that I cooked myself some food; it was a weekend pot. When I did not have everything that I wanted, I had to use what I had. Sometimes you just want to drink on the ship. Then sink it into the pit. We are here talking about that other ship — the friendship. Cut out the bull... it and move. Just living life, like, in a groove.

Chapter 26: Bourne, on Wings of an Old Man

The old man is gone from amongst them, but his departure was not an end in itself. It was the beginning of the discussions, if nothing else. Discussions and querying questions were coming at them from folks who were asking as to what had happened. They had not seen anything like him before. Nor have they seen anything like his way of leaving since. Not at any point ever in their lives. The tornado was standing there in front of their eyes, upright and tall. Just like a man, like a valiant warrior of a man. Spinning away on the rapids while bending back and forth, and sideways like this one, of course. As if it was beckoning him to approach, and then. He did just that, yes, that's what he did. The old man approached the scary-looking tornado, and yet more things he did there and then before leaving to go... Gingerly, he walked up to it. Hesitantly at first, though he might have been. He was turning around now and then and grinning at them. Sheepishly grinning at those who had happened to be standing by. "But, but why?" "Just watching the scene, nervously, to see what was going to happen next to him, my guy. Yeah, that was probably why." At the small end of the tornado, where, at the time, it seemed to them to have been digging a hole deep into the ground near their toe. Deeper, deeper, and deeper still. You know, as it lingered yet more, as seen from the top of the hill. And then. He walked up and right into the hollowed-out inner belly of the spinning channel that pulled him in and took the flight off towards the wide-open skies in front of their eyes. Just like that, he was gone from them, winging the flies. Up, up, up, and away it went, carrying with it the wise old man everyone around those parts had come to know as Capo, the captain. Elsewhere, though, others might have known him too, no? "Yes." But simply as Bauctnumboulei for you. Well, it's not quite that simple if you're trying to call him out from among the crowd on some cold old Tuesday or two. Some might have known him elsewhere as "The old man." Mr. Bourne, and yet some other personas to come, maybe. Others may even be found out later down the line. Until then, though.

The Bournes. Picture this: a house on a hillside overlooking the bay. "Bread and butter paint," I heard them say. Butter is the dominant color here, accentuated by white trims and frames, which is the "bread" here in the bread-and-butter mix. Topped off by a rusty-red roof like that, and this, when not covered over by an overlay of glistening white snow, like this on the booth, no? The window and the carved wooden framework around the L-shaped veranda to the front and right side of the waterfront showpiece of an architectural masterpiece are yellow and white, too. That's the very house where she died. Peacefully. "A heart attack," they had said to me. "Can someone die peacefully from a heart attack?" I was heard asking back, over my buttering bread in fact. Yes. I was having my breakfast. I suppose they can, though, because... Although it was being reported in some quarters that she had died peacefully at home in her rocking chair, the cause of death was a heart attack, as it was being reported elsewhere, so I suppose so. She was home alone. The teacup is still sitting in the saucer with the teaspoon wedged in at the base of the teacup on the marble stone. She had been dead for quite a while, it would have seemed. Several people had reported seeing her sitting there in a white rocking chair, as was the custom over there, I mean... She would always sit there in the rocking chair on a lovely day. Sometimes rocking back and forth, but not always rocking. Like, this time, for example, she wasn't rocking. "I thought she was sleeping." One person was heard saying. But she wasn't sleeping at all, not in the conventional sense of the word to call. Anyway, she wasn't sleeping that way. It was the maid, Madge, of course, it was her, Madge found her there. The rocking chair is still warm, I swear. Mrs. Bourne had lived a long and very full life. She was never accustomed to being alone, but the children had all grown up and would have flown the nest one night. The last of them had moved away mere months earlier, gone far away from the homely mess in the area. She never did particularly get along well with the many other helpers, except for Madge, of course. But Madge was not there on that fateful day; it was her day off from work, so they say. She seems to think that she's responsible for it. "I should have stayed." She chides herself even now. She took the blame for what had happened; Madge will take the blame for anything and everything if you let her. But few, if any at all, are those who will let her take any blame for this one. Not this time, it wasn't her call, that's for sure. There was nothing anybody could have done about Mrs. Bourne's death. Her time had come, and she went, softly, calmly. Even with her shoes on, (me). No fuss, no fight, no hassle. Nothing at all to argue about in a tassel, man. "Just perfect," I heard someone say. It was her call. I saw the laughter painted there on her lips, too, in the hall. It was a good ride out, I'm sure, in her comfortable walking shoes. The same could not be said for her husband, though, you know, for Mister Bourne? Oh! As for him? His departure was a unique, one-of-a-kind, spectacular sort of event of the week. His departure was like a quick prayer in the night. Or more like how things would sometimes happen when the spirit moves, out in a flight. Which was often an occurrence in the Bourne's household, come to think of it, please, have me excused. Where are my shoes? Okay, never mind. The spirit would move very regularly within that home and family, it would seem. With the wife in particular, as seen through these eyes of ours, and his. She seemed to get moved a lot like that. At least as far as it would apply to her and some of the others on the lot, not Mister Bourne, though. Yet, he, too, can be moved, it would seem. By way of a dancing tornado, perhaps, or in dreams. Ranse was the youngest of their children. Mrs. Bourne would have wanted more for her children from the get-go. Much more than she or her husband had had the misfortune of not having. At least according to her, and inasmuch as it coincides with her knowledge, or lack thereof. Lack of knowledge, as it, in fact, was. Her lack of knowledge of her husband's upbringing and worldly preparedness for these and other such things in the house, near the birds' nest, of course. She would have ventured into homeschooling and teaching her children herself. She'd taught them to read and write since they were very young. Contrary to how in those parts and at that time, such things were done. Introduced each of them to the arts, music, even the classics, "Get to know how to use it," she said. She told them to expect something finer from life, and before evening. To get themselves married quickly or be someone's husband or wife, in other words, she encouraged them to stay off the farm. Most definitely, off "the programs." "Stay out of the bottom-scraping and subsistence-wage-paying factories and mines," she said. That's what Richard did, and that's what Crystal is aiming for, and eying. Chrystal is the most beautiful girl you will ever set your eyes upon and behold. Or better for you if you should never, like, never set your eyes on her at all, nor behold her. That's because her mind is the shallowest thing ever, and her heart is icy cold. Ranse was setting out on the same trajectory as his brother, but as fate would have it, life would throw him a curveball, and then another. With his father leaving and all. As for his mother, Mrs. Bourne? Look. Here she is at one of those moments. Watch it all through this little instrument. Mrs. Bourne, look at her there, try not to judge her by what you see or hear. One should never judge people or places by their surface appearances, like me. Many beautiful things and serene people you might come to find out, and even places, no doubt. Many beautiful places, too, tend to have tremendous undercurrents of tension under the surface. No matter how pleasant a place may seem, no matter the tranquil view, even if it appears somewhat like a dream. There are often opposing forces at work, pushing wills one against the other fork. No mention of the grinding corks. Try to discover people and places for who and what they are. What they really are. Can you see her? Can you still see her there? Look, there's the garden on the other side. Imagine you can hear the words, the groaning, and the grumbling coming inside; it's trickling in. She sometimes sounds and looks like a girl when heard coming from there. Or at other times. Even though she might look like a grown woman from afar. It could have been one whose mental growth had not quite caught up with her body when leaning in the car. When you happen to hear her and what's coming out from the inside of her. Sometimes it is hard to tell which of her personas would rule supreme on any given day. It probably depends on which side of the bed she happened to wake up on, one might suppose so, to say, right? But, imagine on. Imagine that you can hear her, you're listening in and hearing her as she's pouring it all out, telling a secret tale to the garden in a language so very much like your own, so that you can understand every word and noun. Now, imagine further. Imagine that you're looking out there at Mrs. Bourne as she is out gardening. Tilling the soil and planting all evening, planting seeds, perhaps. And talking to herself again, and the crops, and singing. Yes, she's singing for sure. Now and then, you would hear the sweet melodies coming in through the door, and the freak ones too, sometimes, coming on through, like rhymes, you poor... And like her, you too, like the mistress, like Mrs. Bourne, I mean. You, too, now feel the need to sing, then you would. At the top of your lungs, or bottom, on the other hand. You, too, would sing. As it has become the norm, she's there and carrying on. "Is she praying? Is the spirit moving again?" I was to hear this coming from him, from the Mister Man. "She has gone up to the temple again, out in the garden. That's her temple, her place of worship." Mr. Bourne pouted at her out there on the warship, I mean, on the garden square, that's it, no? "Yes." She's offering up a sacrifice to the gods, too, and for sure, to the spirits. "The spirit had moved on that very day, I was sure." Mr. Bourne was to swear at this and swore some more. "The mistress was out there in the garden," he said. "She was kneeling too, must have been praying and rebuking you, back to bed. But why? The plant died, didn't it? The one she was praying for, on her knees? Praying to the gods to keep it alive, I mean? So, tell me, why? She's out again today, though, and one isn't quite sure what time of day the clock is striking to show. Is this a time to laugh, or a time to cry?" She often blames the Mister Man for making her do things, to make her have to revert to the garden, even. Said that the mister had a way of bringing out the worst in her. "If I bring out the worst in people," he wondered out loud at the weevil. "Who put such things in them in the first place?" He laughed at this while turning the corner, pumping his fist, and making himself scarce.

Chapter 27: Behold, Bauctnumboulei

There he was, a squeaky clean-cut guy, mid-twenties-going-on-thirties, walking around half-naked on a campus of the university, not having on him even so much as a single ink spot. None other than for the faded-out patch on his hand, his wrist at that. He wears it no more, though, in this natural age of overly-tattooed folks, to show. This, too, was cause for grave concern for many, even you, no? "No." "Okay." Even got himself kicked off the shuttle bus for a time or two, and for reasons he couldn't quite get his head wrapped around anything to do. "Bauctnumboulei is the name," he said to them as he always does whenever he is asked. A difficult name to remember, but an unforgettable face to take to task. "Why would anyone be walking around uncovered in this modern age?" They would gripe and bicker behind him with fists of rage. He was constantly hearing folks saying these sorts of things, yes, they were coming at him, quick, and quicker than he could answer the question they were asking, yes, sit, sit your horse down, and listen. They did not know that this weird-looking dude among them; the mister squeaky friend. With skin as soft and clean as a baby's backside at some point around ten, or a slap on the fat at 10:30 AM. This dude right here is actually "The man" himself. Or more like, "the king" from another world, from somewhere beyond the sunshine and out there in the other realm.

In his world, and as perfect a condition as his body is now existing, as fixed as... Had he been in Cekkoland now like this, he would have been sitting on the throne in that said Cekkoland by now, or at any other age or dispensation since the inception of the Cekko kingdom. This is the Cekko kid himself, in the latest of his many forms and comings. But they didn't know, how could they have known him? Wherever he went, though, turning heads and scrutinizing eyes in puzzlement would follow. Long gone are the days when he would show off his faded-out anchor tattoo on his wrist to those inquisitive, got-to-find-outers. Those who'd dared to ask him, "What's the deal?" He has come a long way and has forgotten more about much more than most people will ever even learn in a thousand years walking these floors. Let alone a flimsy humanoid type of a lifetime, such as theirs and yours. But things get a bit fuzzy sometimes; his memories tend to fade, too. Just like the anchor tattoo there on his wrist was to do, where the mother cone was to be found embedded underneath the tattoo patch on his arrival, out of the abyss. Or out of some such other thing as that, and this. On the day of his arrival, he came in wearing those patches, carrying them along with him into the humanoid realm and in classes on rims, no? No. Nowadays, though, the strange one has become less concerned about what the nosy-nomads may or may not think of him. He tends to stick his nose plumb above his toes and carries on wherever he goes walking, next. The next place he shows up hereafter could be just about anywhere in the entire universal atmosphere, you bet. But yes.

"September morning has always been a hassle around here, buddy. Get with it. I'll tell you this much, though. You can get all the information you want right over there in that building. Just follow your nose and look for the sign that says 'Information.' You should be good to go," he said, then continued ahead. On the go, yes, he was gone long ago. Like, to go bedding down with the chiefest of the foe, on the lit to go bed-down on it, you know, probably. Bautnumboulei had just arrived on the university campus and was having trouble figuring things out, amongst us. He was a foreign student who came in alone, acting on his own account. Meaning, he has done well thus far; he should be okay. Good evening, my star. Everybody gets somewhat fidgety on their first arrival anyway, especially on the first day. He was a rather small man in stature; however, he was a big, big man indeed. His father was a very nice man, too, and the administration at the university was soon to find this out, and was made better for wear by this and every other shout. Although they never met in person at any point during his son's tenure there. He'd managed to make himself unmistakably present in other ways, I was to hear. His generosity knows no limits, it would seem. He does seem to have a great writing fist too, very mean. Not quite unlike that of his illustrious son Bauctnumboulei, come to think of it. Who knew? Bauctnumboulei would have met and fallen head over heels in love with a girl on campus. Heard they had quite a few children and were, at the time of chronicling the story. I heard they were doing quite well indeed, as compared to us, yeah, said Speed. Although he was a very small man in stature, those children of his are all major or minor giants of sorts, Sir. "He never died," it was said of him. At least, not as far as locally thinking folks could say around those parts and at the water fountain drinks, okay? Well, so they thought in those days, he never died. He just got up and left one day after his children were fully grown and had learned how to fly. Or all but one of them was. That was when he got up and left just like a thief in the night; on a rather stormy night, he was gone. Never to show his face there again, not even in another storm. Well, this, too, according to them, and you, no? "No." Seventy humanoid years later, though, and somewhere in another small town nearer to the gate crater. He was to resurface as someone quite different. But unbeknownst to any of them, they never knew how intertwined these and such other things really were before then. After the flood of the century, there were so many displaced and dispossessed people. Some, like families, as well as individuals, were in the vehicle. Many such people were relocated to various other states, regions, and townships. Bauctnumboulei came in among them on cargo ships. But only as a completely new and different person, Mr. Bourne. Mister Bernie

Bourne to them. There he was to start over as someone new, quite different, and unique was his walking shoe, my friend.

Chapter 28: The Macjaceks

Tyrone A. Macjacek is a wealthy man with a big heart on his hands. He never forgets to reach out and offer a helping hand to those who are in need, of food to eat and things to do, said Speed. While learning to read the horseshoe through, to decide on the breed, and surely, Mr. Bourne is a man in need. He certainly did not seem like a threat to him, not to anyone. With his small stature and all. He certainly wasn't the threatening type of person and wouldn't provoke a fearful call. He was relocated to the city after the recent hurricane and flood rains that had devastated the entire city from whence he'd come running into them. He'd lost everything; he arrived there with little more than the clothes on his back. Just enough to keep him warm and to cover his skin was carried in with him, in his sack. "He's surely going to need all the help he can get." These comments were to be heard coming from each one of them around that neck. Although he wasn't planning on giving him, or anyone else, for that matter, handouts. He wasn't planning on that because it wouldn't be proper. Almshouse. But Mr. Macjacek could help, and would surely be able to offer newcomers a chance at a fresh start. So, that was just what he did. He was rather well educated, too, if one was to go by what he had told them and you. He had lost everything in the floodwaters, phew! "Everything" here includes all his documents, such as those of his sons and daughters, Gentlemen. His children and wife, all of them, were smart ah... oops. But he sure seemed cultured. Sophisticated and well-spoken. They liked him a lot. Suits Bernie just fine. Bernie, therefore, went and got a job working there at one of Macjacek's business store enterprises and was said to be doing very well for himself, the same as I did, until...

The Fallout. Upon his arrival, the newcomer, Bauctnumboulei, found a world in turmoil and deep distress one day. The buzzwords on everyone's tongue in those days were: global warming, acid rain, and climate change, yes. There were grave concerns among the humanoids as it relates to issues such as ice melts, floodwaters, earthquakes, wildfires, and the list goes on like that on all of the humming wires. They packed in and piled all the blame on him. It was not his fault, not his doing, though. Not in the direct hands-on sense or use of the term to show. He was the newcomer, the new kid on the block. Beahon was the man before him, and it was at his feet that all of those blames should rightly fall and drop. "Um." It was Beahon D. Vaille himself who had been in on the action. In a bid to get the job done, or even to a fraction. Even at times when Angie was there but not looking on, he was busily hacking away at his plans. He would have called on his many hidden talents and skills to get it done. Skills such as the bratty brute, the stamping tyrant, the pyromaniac, the quiet storm, and the heatwaves. In each of those capacities, this agent would unleash a different form of tyranny on the earthlings' race. Such tyrannies as that, this, and these: As a bratty brute, he would throw a tantrum on the ice way up there near the North Pole that caused the ice platforms to crack, crumble, and roll. Many at the time would tend to point the blame squarely at others, not at him. He was known to be nice and cool in many quarters and by all of them. So nobody suspected him or anyone else like him, who one might have happened to have known. Instead, they placed the blame squarely at the feet of the bad guy. Or on his head, as is the usual norm back home in icy glades. On Cespedoran, for example, that clown, or anyone else who might have happened to be, even remotely like him, you know. Anyone, the likes of that same Cespedoran person who is now on the go, running away from them, no? "Yes, it wasn't me." So, they would keep on piling on the blame. On the head of the vile one, as always, you know it; the bad ones bear the bad name, as is the regular blame game, and the brunt of those blasting canes usually came running after them. Beating the living daylights out of them. Out of their collective blamers' wrath, too. Yes, as always. But according to whom? According to the facts, it was Beahon who would have been the real culprit in most of those happenings to the crops, if not all. Beahon had been the one who was in on the action, secretly. Unbeknownst to them, in a bid to get the job done, you know, the real job? The return of the lost Genodes to the kingdom, home, and the guards. Everything hinged on that, it would have seemed. But only known to himself at the time, and the team around those parts and parting... No one else in the entire humanoid realm would have known this, and that. All other such things were on the lot, Tory pot. He would have called on those talents and skills to work for him. In each of those capacities. This agent would unleash a different form of tyranny on the earth and earthlings alike. All designed, it would have seemed, to get the job done before daylight, that's what I mean. As a bratty brute, he threw a tantrum on the ice way up near the North Pole, causing the ice platforms to collapse and roll. Set solidly in place for thousands of years, this caused it to crack and crumble back down. Shifting icebergs and melting glaciers were the results of that one. As the stamping tyrant, he shook the very foundation of the earth, causing cracks in the earth's crust, and hence. Earthquakes in diverse places, including the very depths of the seas and other such realms as ours and his. Tsunamis and rising sea levels were the results of such things. These things also led to a mass migration of earthlings from along the Gulf's rims. The water never receded from some of the flooded areas. But in all of this, one should never forget the quiz; he was still a good man. A very good man indeed. Don't forget that, sometimes, one has got to be a bit cruel to be kind, said Speed. Like a pyromaniac, for instance, he goes about setting fires. Mostly forest fires in various places on the briers. Places such as those where he was picking up pings from his many scan results that were suggesting that the Genodes were showing up somewhere around those parts of the ponds, or wherever he suspected that the pellets were lurking in the dark. These actions were designed to burn the suspected matter to ashes from the spark. After which, he would then go right on in and process those as-is. All in search of that lost Genode and this. The pyromaniac and the quiet storms would often work in tandem, but not always. When the fire would burn, the quiet storm would fan the flames. Never stops until the job is done to satisfy him in his beautiful, destructive games, thing. Like the quiet storm, however, it seems to have a way of its own and is clever. Therefore, there were times when she would become a mighty hurricane. Just tearing her way through and ravaging the landscape, again. As for the heatwaves, the whole humanoid habitation called Earth, in those days, was beginning to experience an increasingly warmer climate, like dizzying haze, as the eyes had never met, so much so that things were to become unbearable in many regions for the hermits. Warmer weather was being reported across the globe, increasingly so, and down the road. Over yet more time, the glacier started to melt at an even more rapid speed than primes, like in some places. Places where the human eye had not seen in tens of thousands of years suddenly started to become visible to those eyes of theirs. Paths where human feet have not trodden in just as much time, if ever. Those places, too, were slowly starting to become accessible to them and you, my brother. While some of the Earthlings would have seen these new developments as a good thing. Many were sounding the alarm while others danced and sang with him. There were radical weather shifts and more; the rivers swelled across the floor. Large settlements of people had to be relocated. More and more floods were being reported in various regions across the world as they did. Over yet more time, though, along with all the specialized inputs by this agent in several capacities, such as the bratty brute, the stamping tyrant, the pyromaniac, the quiet storm, and the heatwaves. Things then began to take on some semblance of normalcy in many regions. Salmon started to span the mountain stream again, following the lead ones. They were to breed and die there. Sycamore and oak trees grow tall and mighty in the air. Being fertilized and nourished by the meltdown of all these happenings to the ice fish and the fir trees. Just like all of the other trees in the forests, like these, they too grew tall to "rawtid," yes. They, too, would have grown tall and mighty again. And then, over yet more years and the passage of time. They, too, would have died and rotted, then burned in a forest fire, down to ashes. "What was that? 'Ashes.' Stop." That's it right there, my friends, the ashes? It was a specialty of Agent Beahon.

He had sifted through enough ashes in his time and had found enough of the remaining pieces of the Genode pellets he'd thought. It should have been enough to get the job done back home in the lot Tory pot, he brought. Not all of them, though, but enough. So now, this will be a good time for him to close up the shop and get moving on and away from this rock band on the return trip over to the other-sided slot, no? Oh, man! Go. Transported away by way of a fire-on-the-ice eruption up there. Way up there in that place where it appears to us as if it was the Arctic regional spheres, yeah, that was where it'd happened, but now. There's a new sheriff in town. A dude everyone has come to know as Bauctnumboulei, the short and round.

Chapter 29: Smokey and the Warrior Girls

There came another day when all the elders and chiefs were summoned to the palace to meet the king. His chief minister was to be the topic of discussion among them. But unbeknownst to him, unbeknownst to most of them there, even. "What's up for discussion?" They were wondering about such questions. One by one, they came in. Eyebrows were raised when Smokey was not among the first to arrive, as was the custom besides... and yet more. The biggest surprise was probably when they got there and saw who was already there, sitting to the right of the king. Shad was the person already there with him. Everybody knew that trouble was brewing from there, and then. Liam was sitting there, as usual, a bit slumped in the royal chair, with a new gal, no, I meant to say, pal, a new pal. He was at it again, too, biting his fingernails and chew, chew... chewing, yes, he was chewing it. Or pretending not to be, but they all knew him, not me. He was popping his knuckles, but hiding the act because of that. Not wanting everyone to see, pop, pop, pop, popping it in the palm as he switches and swaps hand to hand, pop. But Prince Bauctnumboulei, where is he today? He's not there this time as they were quick to see, and just as quick to whisper and speak it while trying to say... Not anywhere in or around the Cekko kingdom was he to be seen that day, no sign, even. But few among them knew

the answer to it. He had grown quite a lot, too, since the return of the Shadow man to the kingdom and into the palace, that much they knew. That would have been aided greatly by the well-abled Shadow's magic touch. No malice from you, and such. Until and unless the Genodes are found and returned home to the kingdom, though. So that the proper rituals and applications may begin to take place in the boy's life and aid him in his development to fully grow, to become the next king. He still will not ascend the throne, which would have been way too big for him to be able to sit down anyway. This meeting ended dramatically differently from the previous one that was held to discuss the said sorts of delicate matters at a much earlier time of the day. Between them both, Shadow Needleman and the king, now sitting out there on a slow boat, chatting. The new plan was to be put in motion in the end, and coming from among them was this one. The plan to see Bauctnumboulei sent away to sojourn among the humanoid kinds of prey, and to try his hand at some earthly things, too, I'd say. Maybe even to try some things with earthly people, just maybe. Among other things, as may be designed to be put onto the vehicle with the lady. Some sort of setup that would see him meet up with an agent one way or another. He needed to get in touch with another agent and his brother. An agent who is already out there and should be returning home to Cekkoland in the not-too-distant future. Some other things need to be done in the meantime, though. There are still some transactions to complete before that time comes around the corner at Benbow, but then, go. Move over, no?
"No."

Angie is here in Cekkoland now. She's having a love-hate relationship with the place and the arrangements, somehow. Ever since she'd arrived there with Beahon, her long-time boyfriend from the world beyond, things have been changing, but not always to her liking. Things have been changing a lot, yes, but not for the better, as seen from her earthling's perspective on the swap shops of such matters, mi bredda. She hardly gets to see him, and getting together with him to relax and chat about doing this and that was almost becoming a thing of the past.

Which she sure as hell did not bargain for in the talk, and which she did not want. However, she's relishing the idea of longevity of life in Cekkoland. She has calculated that such things will probably balance out in the long run. The people there seemed to be rather nice, too, sometimes. That is, whenever they're not on the kingdom's business, Sunshine. They do seem to take things a bit too seriously at times, in that regard. Or more like, a lot, and all of the time, in the slot in the yard. She has been having a hard time lately, trying hard to get over what had happened to the girls on their special date with him, not me. Yeah! Those girls, her newfound friends and playmates. With what was to happen with the fallout and such, they were just about the same age as her. (Well, so she thought). But, the fallout, their kind of falling-out, bad luck; both through the hole as well as from grace. That thing just hopped up and struck her square in the face. They were beginning to get comfortable with having her as their new Cekkolandee friend, and she? She, as a humanoid being, was beginning to be heard referring to them that way when calling their names. Like, "Hey there, my friends," such and such, but then came the call for them to attend to the kingdom's business again... no, not to rush, to the play. "She's not allowed to go," they were quick to say. Somebody had said that she wasn't done with the process yet and therefore, couldn't go there to stand before the king toe to toe. Makes her suddenly want to start liking the process a lot more now, no? "Yes." After what had happened, oh, how she misses him. She still misses him; she misses Beahon a lot, but what can she do? It's not like she can just pick up her little kitty bag and head home to Mama in her walking shoes and socks. After all, it wasn't all his fault. As for him? Shad was not yet done with his task of trying to get the Genodes and the king's son, Bauctnumboulei, all the way back home to the king. All intact, and to the kingdom, that was for sure a thing for her to grasp. But how did Angie get here, from there? Come along with me, and you will see or hear.

The return of the girls. It's getting dark. Look, the girls are riding back into town, as they had done many times before, while on the ride back from just doing the rounds. Lending a helping hand to the poor sometimes, on the grounds. They're bringing some company in along with them this time. Just like they have done on a few other occasions in the past, too. Yeah, like, as may be seen by every sign, coming to us from friends who knew. The cargo is on the beasts with them. Cargo, yes, as these two were more in a "things" state than a "people" state at this point, I guess. The big ONE: Onella, Noella, and Estella were coming in, homeward bound, to the king and him. Look, look at them, can you see them yet? There's the lead rider, Onella, riding in first. Smoke is still trailing behind each of them as they ride on the wings of the wind, and push-splitting back the color-streaked wind burst with the tree limb. Look, the second and third riders have cargo aboard the beasts, in the form of a man and a woman sitting in the seats. Sitting in front of the warrior riders, yes, but not at ease beside hers. They're not sitting there on each person's account beside the girls' knees on the mount. Those two, the cargo, were not sitting up there on their own accounts, like so, Beahon, for instance, (look at him). He's sitting there, limp, head leaning to one side of the sink near the chair. The rider and pilot behind him had a hand around his thing, there, as she touched up the coupling cup against him. "Where?" There. Look, look. Look at it right here in the recording books, see? Hardly any effort was needed to support him because of the force of the wind against him, not me. It was more than enough to brace the limp body of the seemingly unconscious "other person" there on the beast, and who was up against the rider of the fast-moving beasts as they pierced the rushing wind on the ride in, on the approach into town. Like it has always been with the riding warrior girls, wherever they go, or whenever they come again, home. It has always been in the same style, speedy and stealthy, my gnome. So now they have landed, sort of. Partly landed back in Cekko territory. But surely not empty-handed, no small talk to tell me as the fans did. "Hurry, hurry." Ministers are gathering around and offering some much-needed assistance, like gowns, to both Angie and Beahon. As well as to the warrior girls now on the ground, too, and who must be rushed off to the lab and into the decommissioning chamber, as it was known, by them and you. Among other things, to be done to them, and anyone else who might be coming home, like Beahon and Angie, for instance, yes, those. They were also there to assist with the cargo that the girls had lugged home with them on the beasts. I'd suppose and say this, because they too must be taken to the lab without delay, with no dragging of the feet, I'd say. Meaning, quick. There will be a gathering in the king's court before long, as is the norm. The sooner the king is briefed after returning home, the better for everyone there to get back on their feet and head home to the dorm. The girls will be there. Beahon will likely be there. As for Angie, though, no, she most certainly won't be there; she'll need a lot more time than was the norm in the assimilation chamber. Sitting in the chair, and going through detoxification rituals and reconditioning with the brothers. Those types of wares and tares of theirs need a lot more care, which she most certainly needed to go through to acclimate her to Cekkoland standards over there. It took them much longer than was the norm to get Angie prepared and ready for life, according to those same Cekkoland standards. Probably because of all those tattoos on her neck near the head, and running under her... clothes. But life goes on in the meantime, who knows...? Beahon was, in the meantime, busily hopping around and getting himself carried around from one high-stakes meeting to another. He was fast becoming a kingdom insider, getting closer and closer to the king than anyone could have dreamed possible elsewhere, and wider. He was so close to the king that he was seen living in the palace. Allbeit, in the far corner and almost at the level of the dungeons, but in the palace anyway. I'll trade up with him on any given day. Shadow was a regular thereabouts, too. He'd become a fixture of sorts in and around the king's courts since his reluctant return to Cekkoland and back to you. In the meantime, Smokey was taking note of these, among other things. Hardly anything escapes his eyes and attention in the scheme of these things. But he wasn't the only one taking notice of things around those parts as it was. Others were quick to notice sly changes in that Smokey dude of his in recent times, too, and the collar-hopping bugs. "True?" Yeah, like that one dropping on his shoes from above. "Isn't that what it was?" He became edgy and wore a worrisome countenance, the same as you. Something is bothering him, and it doesn't argue well for the smooth running of things in Cekkoland. King Liam, at the time, was having regular private audiences with the newly returned home Beahon. Oh, how Smokey wished that he knew what was being discussed and what was to be found out, but not so, he was turned away and tuned out of the network feed. He was like everybody else in Cekkoland, yes indeed. In terms of him being left in the dark as to what was being discussed, or what was to be found out. Well, everybody but you, and a few, yes. There were a few others like you who knew, and therein lies the real trouble, too. It was on some very privileged information that Bauctnumboulei would have been sent out into the humanoid world. Info Smokey wished so very much that he had been privy to the girls... Ugh, what's that? He was not. Well, to the girls, perhaps that. But as for this? Now, this is how and where he'd squirmed and hissed, "This is not good, not good at all." Not for him at the very least, and he knew it. King Liam, for a long time, was harboring doubts of some kind. He was harboring doubts that the Genodes would ever find their way back to their rightful place in the kingdom. The longer the mission dragged on, the more convinced he would have become of these things, and that one, especially. Then, upon Shadow's return the second time to the kingdom without said Genode pellets. That was it. That was more than enough to have tilted the balance in favor of another plan; the plan that the king had been pondering for quite a while to furnish a fix, my good man. "If my son is not going to be able to become a normal person. Like a regular Cekko child. Fully grown, fully developed, and in a normal state to be able to ascend unto the throne to reign in as normal a state as any and every other Cekko king before him. If he's going to live on like all of the men in the king's lineage always do. Then..." Yes, it would have been better for his son to continue living in another realm. In another worldly form and point of view. Like, in one of those humanoid forms, perhaps, like that other one who… "Even you, no?" "Yes." That was to be it; that would have been what the king would have ventured into doing as the new task. Or at the very least. He would have ventured into trying some experiments with these fix-bits when he sent him off to go out into the humanoid worlds to live there and learn the ways of the humanoid kind as his new business. The scale had tipped in favor of that move when, upon his return, Shad would have let the king in on some earthly things. Secrets, even, and then some more. So now Bauctnumboulei is there, look, out there in the humanoid world sphere. He's loving it just a little too much for his own good, it would seem to the king and the girls, there. That, if he's ever going to even contemplate a return to Cekkoland and to reign after him. But what was it? What did the Shadow Man say to the king to have him make such a drastic move as that and this? You'd asked? It was more than what Shad had said to the king in terms of their private discussions out there on the terrace behind the drinking glass. The tales that were told of the many escapades he would have had with the feminine types of humanoid kinds stirred the interest of the king for him to have added those things to the mixing tin when coming up with a decision about the future of his son. It was a tradeoff the king was willing to take if the continuation of the king's lineage sitting upon the Cekko throne could become so vulnerable, he thought. So much so that at the wink of an evil eye from the terrible, of a sort. Someone can make a single move that would have rendered their son and heir to the throne incapacitated and lying there up until that day (oh my). In a state where he was hardly anything more than dead anyway. Man! It still makes me want to cry. But then, it occurred to the king. If the boy stood the remotest of any chance at living and reproducing or having anything closely resembling a normal life anywhere else. Even out there in the earthly realm and on the dusty belts, in the humanoid world, that's what he meant. It was a risk that he would have been prepared to take from that very evening. And then… Shad would have broken the news of the toad phenomenon to the king on one of their private little chit-chats. And much, much more than this, and that. The king knew there and then that he had to send somebody out. "What better person than my beloved son, Bauct?" he'd asked. So, that was that. This was becoming a regular thing with them in those times, where they would sit down and chat over a glass or two of wine, and talk they did. They were talking about many and varied things, and the kids all evening. But now! What is this?

Chapter 30: High-Level Hangouts

Back in Cekkoland, a high-level meeting was convened. Smokey was among the last of the movers and shakers in Cekkoland to learn about these things, and hence. Among the last to arrive there in the king's courts, fuming at him, of course. Smokey, just like everyone else in Cekkoland at the time, so it seemed, would have been underestimating the king and his resolve. So, as was the case with all of them, there, Smokey, too, probably thought he could steamroll his way over the king this time again this year. Woo! Like always before. How wrong could he have been? Go, close the door, and sit back down here for a whole lot more than him. Shadow was there, sitting at the king's right hand. Beahon was somewhere there amongst the other guests too, floating around among them and you. But the prince was nowhere to be seen, nowhere in view. And you, where were you? That was among the chiefest of things on the agenda for discussion at the time. Bauctnumboulei was no more, not in Cekkoland at least. Nowhere behind those kingdom doors, eavesdropping on watches and peeps... The king had already shipped him off, unbeknownst to many of those in the park. Including Smokey, yes, since you'd asked, he didn't know about this. Oh boy! He wasn't pleased; if you thought that Smokey was mad before. Well, you're just about to see him go off, and not to the lunatic asylum this time, as you had supposed and thought. It probably would have been good for him if it had been such a place that he was going next, but it was not. Guests were filing in, still. Among them were the girls, not in mission attire this time, if you will. They were casually attired to be there and catching the lustful eyes, the stares, and the spills. So, now Smokey is there in the courtyard, and he's really angry; he needs answers from everybody.

"No, just from King Liam. Say things properly, my good man."

"Okay."

"What is this all about? What is going on here?" He demanded to know. He wanted answers, and he wanted them quick, like, from long ago. If you were there and were like, let's say like, like Angie perhaps. If you, just like her, were a newcomer in Cekkoland, as it occurred, and you happened to witness this exchange as it was going on. You might have been led to think Smokey was the bad man king in Cekkoland, and not sweet Liam. But come on, that was just the beginning of the day's activities. There were a whole lot more things to be seen and to happen than these. Many more things were left to get done and be seen before it was all over with the shouting and be done. "You seemed a bit upset, chief," said King Liam to the fuming, smoking Smokey. Fast turning out around these parts to be seen as a throne thief, and shaking the door key. "Is there something wrong? Is something the matter?"

"Why was I not informed of an assembly? Why am I the last to know anything around here lately?"

"Oh, come on now, chief! Why would you say a thing like that when you know it isn't true? It's you, it is you who is the chief around here, isn't it so? You're the person who gets things to happen around here, no? If you're late getting here, it's understandable. You're a busy man, no? Don't go about casting blame where none is even warranted. Come on in, come on in. Are all of your people with you? Your family, are they all here with you? Come on, bring them in, bring them all in. Where's your spouse? The mother of your son: 'Sparks?'" He was asking this upon Smokey's head spinning around the gaze, and fast, he was flip-flopping his talk too. "As for him, that Sparky... thing." Still asking about these things was the king, against the back-flipping clicks of his finger-ring. "Where's he? Is he with you? And his mother, where's his mother? Bring them in, bring them in." Smokey was to gasp upon the sound of those things; to him, it was like them calling him names, even, and those same people were to blame. He knew at this point that the game was over, and so too was the gig. If he doesn't stand up and fight and win, and that was what he was about to do next, that was the intent: to fight. Two steps forward were all he'd managed to get through in that regard, though, and on that night. "Oh!" Yes, before he was staring down at the sharp end of the snake, hissing firelight near somebody's neck. The serpents that had been lying there dormant for decades, centuries perhaps. There was never a need for such things to pop into life before, I'm more than sure of that. The two snakes that had been there wrapped around the armrests of the king's throne; no one would have made much of them up until then. Aforetime? There was no need to. They were just carvings; intricate carvings on the king's throne to greet you, but not today, though. Today is the day when some dead things are about to be brought to life and make themselves known, and say what they know. Like, what they knew about his son and wife. For instance, just for instance, woo! "Where's your son, Chief Sparks? Where is he?"

"I don't know what you're talking about. I know nothing of a son or anyone by such a name."

"Don't lie to me, Smokey; it's unbecoming of the chief to lie. Not to the king, no, not I." Smokey was hearing this with the sharp end of the snake up under his chin. "Hiss." Oh my! "Again, I ask, where is your son? Whatever had become of him?"

"Nothing."

"Nothing...?"

Meanwhile, some other things were happening in the stadium, and some other people were soon found shaking their boots way down. Amongst them were the girls, who knew? At the height of the inquiry, and in the heat of the moment. Look, here come the girls into the torment. Those girls were walking in there, and they were steeped in the crust of things, too, whether they knew it, or what to do next to fit the new suits. Onella, Noella, and Estella. These three are one, yes, the girls are ONE, as we've already told you. They have always worked together as one. But as for this time? Maybe not such a good plan. They were the very next to have fallen flat under the direct firing line of the king's peace and passivity, I ain't lying, Acidic Alie! As you can see, as soon as Smokey left the scene to go looking for somebody. They walked in. They came walking up to him, casting the blame. It was their turn to bat. Batting more than average to try and bamboozle the king, thinking that they knew him and that he was nothing, really. Speaking of "Know," or knowing. The girls did know quite a bit about things in Cekkoland, it would seem, around the Cekko throne, too, and the king. They were the chief shuttle operators there after all, and prominent members of the shuttle service society too, so I was to hear from you when you'd called. So, whatever happens in the kingdom as it pertains to transportation and other such movements, the girls would have been "in the know" about it. If they're not the very hands-on operators at these events. Or they might be keen to be seen moving along somewhere around the other outfits out there on the pavement. So, for sure, they would have known about the sending or carrying away of the prince, Bauctnumboulei. Or did they? I can't say, not for sure. As things are beginning to turn out around these shores, though. And as for the king, he was done with the playing of the games of the day, and...

Smokey had turned around and was leaving. "Let me go find them," he'd said. "Good evening, I will get them and bring them to you at the said speed," fast he meant, and — "And to bed." "Uh!" But he never left the courts, as he had said. Never went anywhere, other than there. Nor for anyone, other than for them. Moments later, Cekko types of moments to be precise, and greater. Mere moments after the departure of the pauper, some strange other people and beastly kinds of things were to show up there. It was as if Smokey had gone and flipped the lid on the cage, letting it all come popping out on you. He probably did. That was the instant consensus out rear near the back. Those things were mostly women and children that they bore, running in first, and scared out of their crap... Creeping and crawling out of the purse from somewhere, as if on blades. Crawling in, and calling out for things, like papa, papa; my papa, and there, over there, look. There they are. The other creepers, they're coming in too, in the cars, no? no, and children, young children to greet her. Like, babies who are yours, yes? "No." Yes, of course, some of them belong to that guy beside you, too, probably true. But they're coming, too, creeping, even, some crawling in just like the other crawlers. Like those other children, to their fathers, just for instance. Look at them. Some are crying out and calling out, while crawling in and calling yet more for papa, papa, papa. Where's my Papa? But they weren't referring to Smokey this time, in proper. No, not on your dime, nor hers, my brother. They were referring to the king himself, it would have seemed. Some were heard calling for Mama, yes, the mama being too. But no, not at him, nor you. All those creeping things by the scores and other crawling things were coming in too. Popping the locks off many doors to come crawling into view. They were popping up and out from everywhere, and coming in to sneak a stare. Coming in, coming in from the cold, and look over there. There are yet others, I swear, other creatures, coming in on air, and into view, coming in coming in, coming up from the hole, and looking at you. Look, look at that one right there. The one with the big upper and lower body halves, but a tiny halfway marker tied onto the bags. Hop on the way maker. It's there, right there where the waist should have been, but there's hardly anything. Nothing is happening in that region except for, maybe, a binding color-coded ribbon. Which seems to hold the two halves together in unison, or you to the two of them on the wooden spoon. And one is left to wonder, what's the hind half for, Fonda? Because, as opposed to the way it was with Kerre, nothing was happening there. It doesn't seem to bear any load unless it's that type of load. Beware. You know, like, it has no feet to crawl on the road and go there, or come back here. Just there, it seems, bagged and dragged in behind him with things. Must be something precious and special contained therein. But he's coming in yet, and clap, clap, clapping, you bet. Clapping as if asking for the thing he wanted to get. Clapping away with what seems to be some kind of weapon on the front of the plate, there on the tray. I suppose it's to scare everyone and drive them away. One on this side of him, and one on that. With those two, he's coming, and clap, clap, clapping. Must have been a thinker, a spy, or a tailor. As for him and me, yes, I... I'll settle for the tailor. But say no to the sailor. Unless it's to get him to sail on down the fishing line and go sailing away, all along, down to the bay. But as for the tailor, I'll settle that way. A tailored suit maker is where he's at; that's why he's stuck with a clipper and all that clap, clap, clap. Clipping away at some cutting types of claps, and up there above that rock. Look, look at that, look up and overhead. They're coming in too, just as said. Floating in on windy wings with those spinning humming things, to come perching upon you and him. On this side over here, two or three or however many more there may be of them. Those wing-flapping things like vampire bats flying in, but then. Look, see what I mean? An equal number on one side, as well as on the other side. They're floating in on humming tracks, listen, hear that, Clide? Buzzing sounds woo woo woo woo wooing and coming, coming, coming in — "Coming into this dance, no?"

"No, it's not a dance."

"Oh, I must have forgotten about that; what was the chance?" But yes. It's to the king's courts where they were not summoned to come in a-forts. Maybe others were summoned to the door, but they? As for them, no, sir, they were not given an invite, that's for sure. But they're coming in tonight, through the door, as guests. Now we're all there, I mean, here, yes, we are looking up and out. See what I mean? Look, there is one, crawling, moving along on what seemed to be hundreds of tiny legs, hauling them all in. Like him, look, look at him. See those very many legs? No, I don't think so, those legs are too small and moving much too fast for us to be able to see them all at last, as they go. Let alone count them; one, two, nine, and yes, a hundred and ten. But yes, that's how it was to go, that's how it went. Smokey was quickly back, though, back before the king and standing in his presence again, like so. He's an old man now, and the time card may be stacked against him somehow. That may be the very reason why he seems to be taking the short and easiest way out of everything of late. The last nuggets, too, he takes off every platter or plate. Time cards, though, may not be the only thing stacked against him. "Oh?" He has been straddling the fence between the king's business and several other points of interest for a bit too long, it would seem. Playing both sides of the divide in his schemes. Playing the king for a fool, right before his eyes. Liam is a gentle soul; some have even gone so far as to say "he's simple-minded." But be ye reminded, he's not. He seemed to us, at least, to some folks, and on some of the time slots, while riding the spokes. "No jokes." "Holy smokes..." he seemed to have a knack for choosing his friends very well indeed. Knows how to keep an eye on those whom he must keep an eye on in the Indies, or two. Some haters whom he must also live and work with, like you. Even though he knew very well that they may not be too fond of him. One such character thing would have been that said Smokey dude, yes, him, too rude. Some strange goings-on and revelations were building up to a blowout, too. Blowing up and bursting in the palace and around the current Cekko throne, as it would seem to some folks like me and you down home. Around the previous one, too, even. Some people were going to be getting what had been coming to them for quite a long while. Like this very Smokey personality, for example, in his finest style. Smokey was adamant that he did not know anything about what the king spoke. He had no son at all, he'd said, no hope, because he was never married or "certified regular." As if that was a justifiable reason whatsoever. But then, the truth was just about to be revealed by the revealer when... yes. It was to happen when Shadow, yes, that man, Shadow Needleman, who was there all the while sitting beside the king, watching and listening, but never opening his mouth as if speaking. Up until he would have sprung a surprise upon him. On them, on almost every one of them, there and then. The Shadow Man had been sitting there by the king all that time and watching the scenes. Now his time has finally come for action and for fulfilling his dreams, probably. He reached for the container, popped it open in plain air, and pulled the mummified remains of Toady the toad out of it there. Just after Smokey was done denying ever having a son or wife. Or even knowing of any such things, betraying the codes and norms of the knights and the Cekko kings. Just then, Shad pulled the thing out of the container and held it up for everyone to see, straining her and their brains, my dear. "Yes, I see."

"Know anything about this, Smokey?" He was to be heard asking such of him, Smokey. Yes, he'd asked this of the Smoking Smokey Being, that thing. Smokey, in a fit of rage, stomped so very hard, enraged, that the ground beneath his feet would have cracked, crumbled, and quaked, and before he knew what had hit him, he was being humbled as if to the grave as seen on this side of the glade, and going down, down, down. The king, as gracious, kind, and caring as he has always been. Offered him a helping hand to reel him up and in, in the form of a long string flung out to him. This would have happened when he shot the anchoring hooks that are attached to the ends of the binding ropes, kind of chords, over in that nook. Those kinds of chords applied to the kings, the people in their yards, and the good cooks. The types that cannot be cut loose, nor broken hard. "Nor soft?" "No, it cannot be broken at all, my boss." But alas! The thing he shot was quick in coming back after it caught up with Smokey and overtook him. Wrapping around him and rendering him unable to go any further down nor to come back up with it, to sin. So, from that point on, even until this very day, long. Smokey is hanging suspended there, floating around in the outer atmosphere. He's going to be getting some company soon, though. No?

Chapter 31: Back Home, But Not to Sit Down

After the fallout of Smokey, he who would have trampled on allowed things once too many times, yes, no joke, Leigh. He had a falling out of sorts, of his very own, this time. You know, falling out of the hole and from the throne he'd climbed. But chiefly so to speak of these things sweetly. From the very hole that had opened up beneath his feet, Leigh, to the ground. Yes. That's it. Shadow pulled out the container and popped the lid open, while Smokey was there, denying and smoking. Like lying to the king, even. That was when he'd popped the lid on the container open, and out came the toady-toad corpse of what was once Smokey's spy insert of sorts into the humanoid world. He was also an agent and a son. A son whom he had sent out to do several things, not just one. The very same son he was there, moments earlier, denying as he lied to the king, saying that he had no son. Among other such forbidden things that should not be done, ever. Among the tasks, Toady the toad was commissioned to perform, as was to be found out much later on his a… well, as was to be made known there that day by way of the announcements to everyone. He was supposed to follow the agents around. Real Kingdom agents, as they were known: Follow them around and take note of their every activity. Disrupt every plan or move that they would make in trying to find the Genodes, not me. So he was told by the bag of bones wearing old clothes. "Oh, Gee." Therefore, whenever the agents would have been closing in on a sighting of any of the Genodes. The toad would go in first and remove it, and place it as far away from reach as possible, and from under their sniffing nose, Mr. Hustable. Before the agent could get there and cause him some trouble. Furthermore, Toady was charged with the additional task of keeping the chief up-to-date on everything he would find out. But he was stopped in his tracks in that regard and closed his mouth. Shad would have caught up with the toad in the wilderness just before him, being snatched away again by the wonderful comings and goings of the fighting girls, and brought back home to relax and sit down with his counting of pearls. It was to be someone else's task to finish him off, though. Someone else eventually managed to finish the job. The job that Shadow had started with the toad. Shad, for his part, doesn't know for sure at this point who it was that had done it, or how fast. Some facts would have gotten lost on him while he was in transit, back home to the boss. Bautnumboulei probably did, or Beahon. Most likely him? One of them did, though, or both, as far as he was able to find out, or get to know on oath. But it was him, yes. It was the Shadow man who had started the process of taming this wild thing. Among other wild things he was out there doing, like those other things he was chasing after and roping in. He, the Shadow man, though, was done and gone back home on the row. "Oh, no?" "Yes, Bro." He was sent back home to Cekkoland to relax and sit down before he could finish the task by himself in top form. But he would have informed the king and his best friend, Liam, of all these things upon his return home. The king, therefore, having been armed with that knowledge and more, would have tasked his son when he had to send him away in the carriage. Bautnumboulei was tasked with doing some things and with getting words to the next agent out there in the fields, about what to do to get to the toad and put an end to its activities. But then, here we are, again.

There was yet more shaky kneeing to come over there in Cekkoland, and home. Among those things and people were the women, their vehicles, overloads, all of them, not just one. Look, look at them. Come on in and look at the recorded flashbacks, get to see it as if it's just happening here now in the park, as it was happening then, way back. It was the girls' turn to spend their time with the king. Or before him, before sweet king Liam. "The gentle one." Straightaway after those things, like, after the events with Smokey and the king. The girls came in and found themselves standing on the edge of a major breakthrough of their own. At least one of them was not doing the break dance, breaking out through that very same hole through which Smokey had fallen into a trance, and was hanged up upon the response to his advance. Yes, he was hopping up and in, trying to get into his pants for... But old habits, just like so many have said in a fit of rage. "Old habits tend to die hard," over near the wall end of the yard, on the bed. "Oh lord!" Yes, that's what I heard someone say, right there and then. Therefore, it was not long before they would have forgotten about the old boy Smokey, how the chief priest had found himself raising the standards to match up with his very high calling in the outer stratosphere. Or more like falling in there from a much higher place in Cekkoland air. The girls would have forgotten quickly and pushed their luck with the king just a bit too far onto the bixi. To go riding on the ill-figured cross-bar space with him and her, yes, she. And much too soon after those things were to be. "Is there any truth to the story?" The king demanded. "Which of you has been playing the fool?" He would have commanded an answer from them against the tool. The girls were found to be there choking hard on their attempts at answering any and every one of the king's questions, and then. There were other noticeable happenings in the king's court. Girl number two, Noella, for you. The fiercest among the fighting girls is obviously on the brink of having a fit doing the shakes, yes, with that fella wearing suede shoes and shades. She was scared stiff out of her tunic. No, it wasn't just her, Henriquez. All of them were standing there and were frightened. The girls, all three of the fighting girls. But none more so than Noella, and yes, she was about to get a fit fit fit. Or was it...! Oh sheet! Look at this. There was a need for explanations for it. Like, a need to learn how to make a hit like a real Cekko bandit, and as to why those children were calling the king papa, and that is because... If a woman should happen to bear the king's child, improper, though it might be. That child would have been subject to the kingdom's standards and would have been raised as a prince or princess, like me, in style. In the king's presence, no less, and in the palace, of course, my child. Furthermore, it should never happen that the kings' women of old should go on to lie to him, or lie in the other dens behind his eyeskins. Like lying yet more and going about lying themselves down with other men as if they're really friends. So, there should never have been a situation where the kings' women of old times should have had any child whatsoever, calling her mama unless that child was also the king's child in proper. He was to command her attention on the matter. The women over there, though. They would tell everyone about them, so those children were all told that the king was their father, and in fact, some of them were... out of order. There were some strange goings-on and revelations in the buildings, and some were building up to be revealed in and around the realms of the current Cekko throne, it would seem. And the previous ones too, for many generations down, as was to be seen. Some people were going to get what was coming to them for quite a long while. No, not you, I'm sure, but some like these that are about to come popping out next, from under the tile. Or as it was heard coming out of those who were there, arguing in style. "It wasn't our fault," they had said, it was Smokey's. But on this day? It was he who was forced in through the door skin without the door key. He then forced himself upon us. Upon all of us, and she, Noella, was the unlucky one to have gotten pregnant and ended up with a baby out of it for that fella, not me, but him, yes, he, that smoking Smokey is the father of Sparky. We told him "no," and that it was not right and that such things ought not to happen, ever. But he would have none of it. He would not listen to us whatsoever. He forced himself upon us and threatened us with all manner of sanctions, and his brother. We did not want to be prevented from serving the great one, you. Our great king, King Liam. So we kept it quiet, trying hard to avoid a riot. We resisted him with all our might and for as long as we could, but because he was much bigger and stronger than we would... he prevailed over us. But Smokey wasn't there to answer any of it at the time because... "What! He'd bitten the dust?"

"No, not that, but..." He'd hopped out of town for a short spin around the block, gone for a ride on the newly refurbished transport line on the bus, stop, look, listen. He should be swinging by again soon. In the meantime, though, the king had seen and heard enough of them, and you all, no? "Yes," ...and since he's done with getting the ball on a roll, he might as well continue with the house-cleaning call. So, "Go right on in," I heard someone saying, "Your king is waiting."

"Since you and Smokey have already got more than just a small thing going on here," he said, making it clear. "Why not go hang out with the dude, my dear? You should be okay with him. He's a very skilled and qualified camper."

"Please, please, please," and yet more pleasing like these, they were pleading on their knees.

"You know," said the king quite calmly and inquisitively, like so. "It's unbecoming of the king's guards, kingdom warriors, even as you are, chief errand runners of the evenings, too. It's unbecoming of you to go about begging."

"Please remember our long and loyal services to you, to the kingdom, and to your son Bauctnumboulei, the king's son and prince." They were to say this to further stir up the king's wrath and then some more under his skin. "Where's my son?" The king was heard asking this one. "Now, my son, Bauct. Where's he?"

"There, there, out there." She squeezed out this reply over the pointy finger in the air.

"Who was it again? Who was it that had sent him there, yes, to that place?" This was asked with the point of the sword pressed up against her pallet. Right up there under her chin, near the face within. Yes, right there. "Do you still want to test my resolve?" "No, no." "No? Just as I thought," said Liam. The alleged father of all three of them, the girls. Now, at this point, Shadow was beginning to think that maybe one of them was, in fact, the boy's mother. Look at that, my brother! Just as it was told to him in gossiping talks along the border. Could it be? Is that what the king is trying to ascertain from you and me? What strange turn of events are these, I now see? Meanwhile, the serpent that had been there wrapped around the armrest of the king's throne was to come alive again. Stretching itself out, and was to be seen hissing venomous Thongs at the girl's nose, all of them. The glistening sword was coming from the place of the lions' tongues. The lions had also come alive again, at the same time as the two snakes, my friends. The king was certainly not out to play on this day, and somebody was going to be made to pay. One of the girls, probably. Or two or three. Or even you, no, not me. I'm from among the extraordinary. So, while everyone in Cekkoland had thought, or was led to believe, that Smokey's son was by one of the chambermaids, since that was the most popular story around there in those days. It wasn't so, no. He had gone all the way into the king's household, in fact, all the way in, to go and unpack. And was found there reaching out for the goal, and lusting hard after the gold. He meant business, it would seem. But today was to be his day to come clean. Or was it? When all was said and done, he was gone, and the girls? As for them, two fighting girls were all that they were to have gotten left there, to remain. One was not, and it was because of that. "Because of what?"

"Because of the snakes, as well as the lion's glistening sword near the stakes." The snake was zooming in on the girl in the middle. "Oh my Lord, why?" Such a riddle to go try because she was to be favored with the other going down of the day, by way of the same route by which her beloved Smokey had gone away. Yes, by the ground-breaking way, and she was not to be found kicking and screaming much this time, as was the norm, since the feet were to be the first thing going in and be gone. Even before she knew what was happening, out there on the lawn. Don't go a-playing with the king—King Liam. "The gentle one." Or one might come quickly to the realization that he is really gentle indeed.

"Where's Bauctnumboulei now?" He asked. "Who put him there?" The king shot back at them upon their answer, or more like, upon their non-answering. No such good one was to be found coming out of any of them. "Do you still want to test my resolve?" These words were heard floating up and over the hill at the stalls. "But I I, I'm your daughter, will-will... will you please, please, please."

"Please don't please me anymore," he said before... Yes, before that. Before she felt the earth moving under her feet, near the rock. And then, that was when she took the plunge to go deep, deep, deeper into the relationship with Smokey "The sweet." The in-keeper who was already there, and her long-time baby daddy, unfair, though he might have been. She's headed down to go and shack up with somebody, like, with Smokey on a more permanent basis now. Floating around somewhere on the spaceship, like, wow! That dude must be bursting at the seams with his joy bells ringing and all. Smokey has finally got his queen to come over and hang out with him on a long string to call... Sorry, I meant to say, on a long-term basis, of the day, yeah! at the "day's inn" hall, okay! In a jiffy, they should be making themselves very busy working on replacing Sparks, the son they didn't have. But they were to lose him too, to hard times, and Cekko-type bargains of sorts, near the shrines.

They thought Cespedoran had grabbed the Genodes on the way out. But did he? Not as the records were to have shown later for them to see and shout out, with glee. The real records, that is. Those that only the king himself has access to. Or, only upon the king's instructions, would anyone else have access to them. Except. You know, except for... and on this particular exceptional "except-access day," access was given out that way. And look at what we've found!

There were many comings and goings there that day because... Some of those creepy, crawling things came up from behind them, where they were out to play and arguing. Look, there they were, standing in front of him and arguing, or trying out their new tongue at arguing with the king. It wasn't working at all, not at that time. Even some who should have been standing there along with the rest of the standing kind, in the natural and normal schemes of such things as they're known regarding human kinds of beings. They were found crawling. Crawling up and calling for Papa and Mama. At least one of them was calling for Mama. But Mama would have been a quick goner. Gone in the next wink or two, the very next wink of some terrified Cekko eyelids, even, at you. Or was it that thing, the "terrified eyelids, rapidly blinking?" Was that what had featured in her going away from the cribs? Going the way of the ground-breaking fallout of the day? The same way as how Smokey was made to pay and then go away? As much as it would apply to "Mama?" Was that what had featured in sending Mama away, too? No dead and mummified toad-come-to-life has any business at all calling a princess, the king's own daughter, no less. A dead old toad-of-a-child-come-back-to-life calling her mama? Got to go, dear, go where? Out there. Can't stay around here nummo, I mean, no more, as in saying, not anymore.

Shortly after the fallout and falling away of his. The same fate would have befallen that one, that is. The woman who was discovered to be the mother of his son, Sparky. The same son whom he had denied having or knowing anything about, falsely. That woman, as it turned out, was, in fact, one of the king's very own daughters: Noella. Look at that, she was also one of the three fighting girls, and errand-runners going to and from on errands around the world. She, too, was about to feel the earth moving under her feet. Then she would have received the same tender treatment as Smokey "the sweet" did mere moments earlier, isn't that neat? So now, the two of them are still hanging out together, somewhere out there in the stratosphere, and sunny weather. So I hear. After these things, the king issued a command for someone to establish a new commission. Charged with the task of finding all those (supposed) children of his, as well as his father's, and all of the other kings before him in their proper orders. That was the mission. "Find and verify those claims," he had said to them, and if and when those were proven to be the case. These very children must be redeemed and elevated to their rightful royal status, as you know them around this place. And be brought into the kingdom to live and reign with him, and grow. And yes, as you might have guessed (or not). There were many such children, brothers, and sisters, too, on the lot. As the records and inquiries were to be shown to me and you. The remaining two fighting girls, though, are Onella and Estella. They were to be decommissioned and sent off to live in the common space, as common folks. Common Cekko folks, which then rendered them more susceptible to expiration. As for the others, like the Shadow Man. He was taken into the king's highest chambers and given more power than any other Cekko person of no royal lineage before him. He's now sitting on the king's right hand and is reigning jointly with the king in the land where the kings "never die." They adore him. Right there in Cekkoland, upon the height. As for Beahon? He became the new chief in command.

Chapter 32: The Wilderness Meet-up

So, as far as such things were to go, down there in the Shadow man's row. Even now that he's back in his homeland of old times, and is residing in the kingdom with him, closer to the shrines. Although all of those other events in which he would have participated royally are all perfectly well done for him. He's having trouble, great trouble more, of his own. The trouble is with the concept of his rightful place in the scheme of

Cekko things, near the throne. Many are the days when he would much rather be with her. With them, even. Anyone, or even all of them. No matter which side of the great divide, it was going to happen, as long as he was with even one of the humanoid kinds of women. Jay's daughter — Mona, preferably. Or Elsie. Or anyone from among the many. After having Beahon back there in Cekkoland with his lover woman on his arm, that's helping him in the matter none, sound the alarm. Jay's daughter would have been one of Shadow's sleeping beauties who had bitten him the hardest, probably, while he was out there not doing his royal duty. But had gone off course and chasing after... somebody, like these, yes, them. They would have met on his first arrival there. What's her name again? Mona, I think, or something like that, so I hear. But he was dragged back home to rekindle the fire in the kingly realms. That was when he had to run and pass her off to the old man to befriend. But he, too, is now gone. "True." Just because he had to move on and away from you. She was that kind of woman. Unforgettable, she was like that. Once she bites you or me, you may stay fat, or you may go flat. But you won't ever again be found unbitten, you know. Whichever of the two vices you may choose to do. Or even if you're to chew on the rice seeds as food, out of the wooden spoon. As it is written, Shad had lost a little piece of himself to each of the women, but this one? She took the cake, took it right out of the plate. The chest plate that is. They'd forgotten to treat the Shadow man against such things. You know, against the acting up of the wild bugs that tend to inhabit his bloodstream and feast on his nervous system. They'd forgotten to treat him before sending him out on the latest mission. The Bauctnumboulei pellet search and recovery mission, again. It's too late for that now because Shad is not about to opt for that cow, with calves, which might well be the remedy. Not for the risk of wasting the sweetness of that malady. It's way too sumptuous a thing for him to go a-wasting. Not after having gone out of his way and a-tasting, the axillar of love which would have bitten him. It's still biting him really hard there under the crust of his skin, by way of the feminine kinds of earthlings. Even now that he's back home in Cekkoland, he is resisting with everything else that he has got within him, and at his command. "Anything other than bugs that can really punch up a sting on your arms?" Yes, sounds a lot like him. Now, come on. He's fighting it with them, trying to prevent them from applying the solvent to him. Not on their lives, they're not going to. Not without them breaching the sharp end of the knives, the blunt bumps of kicking horseshoes. Or even the squeaking noise from his screaming snooze. They don't know how it feels, and of course, they could never have known, since they haven't loved as much as he has. Haven't loved who he has. Especially those who are there trying to fix him, trying to unsettle him, and disrupt the smoothness of his thick skin. They sure haven't ever really, really, really ever loved a woman. So tell me now, how could they even so much as know? Let alone understand?

The wilderness meet-up. As for Beahon? Here's how it happened at that time. While Beahon was there, busily traveling the humanoid world and doing those things. Like, mapping out the locations where the Genodes were showing up, and tracking them down hand in hand with his girl, Angie, and them, as he knew he must. At the same time, he was linking up with the elders and vanguards of the tattoo art form along the way. It was at one of those times that he was to make the detour. That was when and where he met up with him, and more. As it so happens. It was to be Bauctnumboulei himself. Bauctnumboulei had been sending messages to Beahon for quite a while before. Because they had to meet up to discuss the kingdom's business and to get it done, and get back to his place and to the regular tasks again as quickly as possible. Bauctnumboulei had for a long time been carrying around a couple of messages from the kingdom with him, which were to be delivered to Beahon during his lunchtime, while eating. Or to any active agents who would have been on hand to receive them at the time, but... The only such Cekko agent out there at the time was Beahon. At that particular time, he was preparing to go home to Cekkoland. Though unbeknownst to anyone in the earthly realm, not one. Not even Angie, his girlfriend. So, they met in what turned out to be one of their favorite places in the Earth realms. In the wilderness, as the case was, deep within, where humanoid kinds have hardly ever been. But as for them both. They had no trouble at all getting there for the meet-up and then back out again, as the evidence was to have shown. Bauctnumboulei was rather impressive at his art, too. After all, he wasn't too meager in what he did, furnishing the hall for you. He had to perform a skin graft on him. After Beahon was done with the same type of operation to remove the cone from under his skin, where it was implanted on him for transportation out, you know. But then it had to be re-implanted onto Beahon's person for the ride in, no doubt. He did that very well indeed. Not only that, but Bauctnumboulei also had on his arm some other special cargo he had to hand over to be transported back home to Cekkoland on the border, for the eyes of the king and his inner circle, the household, and those in command. Earlier on, Bauctnumboulei would have caught up with another agent. The most secretive of Smokey's private agents. He performed some magic of his own on it. He had to get some things fixed, using some of the king's kinds of bits taken from his journey kits. As for that and the retrofit, the fix was done as far as he was concerned. The rest must be done in Cekkoland, nearer to the throne. But as for Beahon, his new and additional mission from then on was to get the special cargo back home to the king. Back to King Liam from his exiled son, Bauctnumboulei, for him. As far as it applies to them and to what they were able to do over on the earthling side of the divided realms? Mission accomplished, I couldn't have lied to them. Beahon can, therefore, return to the task at hand once more. His chief task was finding the lost Genodes and getting them home and off the roads. As for Bauctnumboulei, though? Who knows?

Bauctnumboulei was alone then, exiled from his newly found experience living life as an earthling. He was doing quite well for himself, one might say. As an earthling, he was well-educated. He would have been educated at some of the earthlings' most prestigious educational institutions. Went on to marry a fabulously beautiful woman of the humanoid kind, too, to have his few sons. Would have fathered many children with her. And you? "No." Those children amounted to ten. Each of whom he had was to shade his eyes and bend the neck backward to look at their standing faces, so I hear. Don't go quoting me on this, please, I'm scared. But they were all giants of sorts, and smart, even by Earthlings' standards, and in the arts. He would have done very well in terms of earning his keep in the humanoid world and was just about entering into the phase where, according to Earth standards, over there. He would soon be receiving what they referred to out there as "A pension," or some other such thing to quench them. It was just about this point when he got up and left. Just like a prayer at night. "From among thieves?"

"You bet," without a fight. He has not been seen by any of them over in those regions, again, since. At least not as would have been made known to them over welcoming rum drinks. Not in ways that they were aware of or could articulate and refer back to. No, but as for him, he saw them all, most of the time. "Yeah?" "Yes, that's true, I'm not known for lying." He has been busy, though, looking out for their greatest good too. All be it unbeknownst to them, and you? After the meet-up with Beahon that evening. Bauctnumboulei lingered on in the wilderness for quite a while longer. Just passing the time away while meeting other people down under, and getting his feet wet, with hunger. Floating around the spheres of those said folks there, and others offering him a helping hand, such as the Macjaceks, yes. Getting in just a bit too deeply with them, too, before he had to leave from there and go away, anew. He then journeyed in quarters across many waterways, across just as many borders, and the likes of those, among the stowaways. Before he arrived in the Americas and settled there to begin a new chapter in his life off the roads. To live with them and us in this chapter of his life, on the globe. Which was to see him existing there in the personality of Mr. Bernie Bourne, and his wife.

The tornado was just standing there, upright and tall, I hear. Like a man, a valiant warrior of a man. Spinning away rapidly while bending back and forth, and sideways like this one, look, there it is over on your right hand, of course, as if it was beckoning him to approach the highways just this once, and then he did. He would have approached. Gingerly, he walked up to the tornado. Hesitantly at first, though he was. Turning his head around now and then, and grinning away at those who had happened to be standing by with their necks bent, just watching the scene. At the small end of the tornado, the most dangerous end of it. According to humanoid views on these and such other things, to quit—"As it was said by that one looking at them while on the way to go and nyam...?" "No, not that one, but she, the one that was going to eat something." The end that, at the time, seemed to them to be digging a hole in the ground. Deeper, deeper, deeper, and round. And even deeper still, as it lingered yet more, and then. He walked up to it and walked right in. Into the hollowed inner belly of the tube-like spinning channel that pulled him in, and took the flight with him, off towards the wide-open skies, just like a kite. A kite cut loose from the supporting string. Up, up, and away it went, winging the flies. Carrying with it the cool dude everyone came to know over there as Bauctnumboulei. He then became Capo, the captain one day, Mister Bourne among the stowaways, and yet more personas of him were to come, as may be found out later on, too. There may yet be more personas of him to come before he returns home to them and you. As for these and other such things, and how they were said to go. There were many players down there below. Shad would have wandered around in the wilderness and other such places and would have gotten into more trouble than any one man had any business getting into. Even if he were to have been one of the humanoid kinds and acted as we do. Which he was not, Shadow was an outcast of sorts. He was cast out from among them, in almost the same manner as Cespedoran, the vile one, was when... Yes. Cespedoran was cast out at an earlier time, and for quite a lot of devious reasons. None of which Shadow was even remotely guilty of, or was accused of, by Stephen. But he was cast out anyway. Cespedoran, though, was cast out for thieving and treason. Oh? But not before he would have gone further and stolen some more of the kingdom's most precious treasures.

For no apparent good reason, none whatsoever. As the story still goes on over there, he was accused of stealing Genode pellets. They were there, in the place where they have always been. But then, upon their waking up, heads spun, somebody was quick to notice that Cespedoran was gone, and so too were the pellets from under their hands. All of them. So, "Where the hell are they? Where are they now?" Frantic and petrified, the then-ministering servants were scrambling for an option as to what to do next, other than to run away and hide. The pellets were designed to be gradually applied to the young prince throughout his formative years. From birth and on through the adolescent years and into manhood, as was the custom over there, concerning all of the kings, but they were gone. The pellets were all gone, supposedly stolen by Cespedoran, "The vile one." Those pellets need to be returned to the kingdom. The ministers all knew it. They must be applied to the young prince to restart the process to get his growth, development, and maturity back on track and moving again to go and do it in the element. But alas, thanks to him, they lamented in the talks. "Thanks to the vile one." The very young prince's growth, development, and progress have stalled. All of them, for the most part, had concluded that Cespedoran was the culprit in that. "What shall be done now? What good is the rest of my life? Mi blow-wow!" So mumbled the chief minister through trembling lips there that night. As of yet, the king, King Liam, the father of Prince Bauctnumboulei, was still unaware of those things at this point. But it wouldn't have been much longer until he was brought up-to-date on this matter, in the joint. So. Shad went twice. Beahon went once but took Angie back home with him. Along with the information that was going to change the course of life and many other things in Cekkoland, for many. From then on and moving on. That was to come about with the showdown that followed and its aftermath. At that time, Beahon and Angie were there looking on. That's when they were to discover and see what was to be sent over later on for me, to call it all mine. They'd noticed that it wasn't as it was said in practice. But it was Smokey who had seized the Genode pellets and stuffed them in his pockets. "Who knew?" He's said to have seized them all at some earlier point in time, as the story goes. Then gave some of them to Cespedoran on his parting, out the doors. So, it was not all Cespedoran's doing. Or any at all, even, as was to be revealed later that evening. Toady the toad, though, yes, him. Toady was sent in to disrupt the process. He was constantly pushing them away from the coveted prize. Or it, away from them, as they were going towards the house-dresses. Anything at all to disguise, or to sidetrack their eyes on women, for example. So, no matter how long those agents may have been out there in the humanoid world and searching. Or how hard they might have tried, I'm more than certain, they would never have been able to find them all. Nor to bring them in on a purse-string back to call, because they were never all there. "No?" "Yes." Trust what I say, because I say so, you hear. Yeah!

Chapter 33: A New Day Has Dawned

After all these things, Bauctnumboulei would have skipped town on the wings of the wind and left. Leaving his wife and family. Well, his children had all outgrown his house and home by then and had moved on to start their own families and to seek to find their way in the world. All but the youngest of them. He wasn't completely gone yet, but was always in and out of there. He, too, will be gone for good, though, soon. Bauctnumboulei was said to have left his wife at home at the time and has not been back there since. After that, according to the gossip around the kitchen sinks and the steamy boiling pots. He met up with Beahon and they made some transactions there amongst themselves, then they parted ways and went their separate ways. He then lingered and languished yet a few decades more in the wilderness, away from friends as he did, yes. Also meeting other people, and doing other things with them, getting his new kids to do evil, as was the custom. Like, getting into more mess, before he resurfaced in the Americas to undress, sorry, I meant to say, unpack. To unpack and start his life over, another of his earthly lives, living it outback as Mr. Bernie Bourne. But his wife...

She was there, hanging out the laundry on the clothesline, the laundry she had been washing all morning, and feeling uncharacteristically so, you know, like, sublime, and upbeat. Not that she wasn't an upbeat and jovial type of person, to begin with. No, it wasn't that, but this. More like, she had never felt this energetic and upbeat after having washed so many dirty clothes in one sitting. Not even getting any help this time from her sister, Jarden. But she was nonetheless upbeat and spirited. She was humming a little melody from deep within when she looked up and saw him coming, approaching from the southern end of the lonely gravel road, leading in. Usually, folks would have been more likely to be seen going the other way at that time of the day. Going to work, most likely, to earn another day's pay, they would have been coming back this way in the evening, heading for home with the feeding that the family would need. But this one person, this individual, is coming north towards her. He's got her attention, that's for sure. He's coming still; his bodily outlines are becoming more pronounced. His fantastic features are more discernible now. She had not seen such a person around these parts before, she was sure. At first, she thought it was a young boy because of the small frame. Dampening the initial joy and dousing the flame. The body size seemed more suited to a child than that of a grown man, but all of the other bodily features spoke rather loudly to her senses that this was a grown man. "Not from around these parts, I'm sure." She reasoned such from within her bore. "Around here," she said, "men are men and boys are boys, but..." as for this one. He's still coming, much closer now, and she's still doing what she's been doing there. Washing and wringing out the clothes with strong, powerful arms like those. The arms of a country type of woman I'd supposed. That of a strong farm-country type, of a woman, still, full of homely charms. "One of the good ones." She's wringing the clothes almost dry before hanging them out on the clothesline to dry, really dry that is. Drying out what's left of the water residue in them after her strong-arm wringing and squeezing. Ten minutes under the heat of this morning's sun, they'll be more than perfectly dry and ready for her to bring them in. To go inside for the next one, the next tender treatment, ironing. It wasn't a mere coincidence that she was there hanging out the clothes on the line as the stranger came abreast of her, where she was, and eyeing him. It was deliberate; she wanted to be on her feet when he got this close to delivering it. Just in case, you know, and that is where she is now, on her feet. And he... look at him, he's so sweet! He's just about to greet her, so. Listen up while you continue looking on and eat hers. "Dore-fish?" "No.

"Howdy, ma'am."

"Well, hello there. How are you? Are you from around here, no?"

"No, just passing through."

"Well, want to sit down and rest your feet awhile? You looked tired—yes?"

"Yes, ma'am, yes, thank you."

"Care for a drink, something cool perhaps, you must be thirsty—yes?"

"Yes, please, some cool water would be nice."

"Coming up, you just wait right here, I'll be back in a jiffy."

It was as if she were telling him the answer she wanted, the correct answer. Her correct sort of answers, as she sees fit. Now, look at this. Look at her as she goes. Going, still going. Going up the three-rung stairs now, to the back door. She's pushing the door open. Careful now, don't let her catch you looking, she might see you looking at her as she's constantly turning and looking back at him, still standing there, and you? What are you doing here? He's leaning a shoulder up against the stick, the stick he had dragged in with him. Or was it the stick that had dragged him in with it, to sin? Anyway, he's here, and... She has gone inside now and is out of sight. "Right." The young man is looking around, searching for something to mop his brow, bright, or brown, well, maybe. He seems to have found it, oh, no, it's not that, the cloth! It's a smooth piece of board of some sort, he has rearranged it somewhat and is now sitting on it and preparing to lift his feet and kick you in your ho... oh no, won't bother with that, but... "What, why?" Because he wanted to finish what he was about to start, Ms. Vye. Settling himself down now, back up against the tree, that same tree that is supporting one end of the clothesline and him, not me. Slowly, he's looking around, his eyes scanning the scene. She's coming back, with a large jug of some sort in one hand and a drinking glass in the other. Another woman is hopping along behind her elbow. They're communicating, in hushed tones, in whispers. Saying something of the unknown, to him, yes, to the mister. "Look at you, you seemed a lot better already, sit-sit, sit right back down, and relax." He was fixing himself to get up and greet them on the approach, but she was rather forceful in the command for him to remain seated. So, he did. "This is my sister, Jarden," she said. "You know, I just remember to ask, what is your name?" "Berb-berb, Bernie," he said nervously. As he was heaving himself up somewhat. Supporting his weight with his left hand as he offered them both the right, in a swap. "Hi Bernie," she said quite chirpily, yes, the other woman, Jarden. Jarden sidestepped her a bit and popped herself out from behind her sister's abyss, I mean, from behind her sister. With an outstretched arm, she said, "Hi," to the mister, "nice to meet you, Sir." Meanwhile, Meighen, the elder of the sisters, who was the first of the two women to meet him. "Jarden's sister," as she was known to him up until this point of the evening, and even beyond. She still didn't give him a name. However, she was quick to hand him the drinking glass after he was done greeting them both, just saying. "Here, have some of this, you look really parched — no?" "No, I don't need an excuse to drink a cold one with my crew, I mean, with people like you. Or do I?" He was musing about this with them, upon the misty, smiley glint from the eye, beckoning her to come in and try. They laughed. He reached up a heavy right hand from where he'd sat back down before taking the drinking glass. It was cold to the touch since you'd asked. He hesitated for a brief moment, looking in the glass at the water before lifting it to his thirsty lips and sucking cool, clear water in like a glutton, ish. The sisters just stood there watching him. Staring at him as if it was "nuttn," I mean, nothing. "So, where are you off to?" She queried him again, as she was walking away on a soft shoe. With her back towards him now, but not stopping from looking over her shoulder at him. She'd turned around and was walking back to where she was sitting before, and washing. She's washing some more, squish squish squish, squish squish squish, squishing away with her hands like this, washing the clothes. Flashing him the occasional full-fledged glance now and then as things were to go. But Bernie knew that she was watching him continuously, like, like from long ago. But as for her? Jarden was still standing there by her side, her arms still folded across her breasts, as if to hide... it. Trading glances back and forth between Meighen, her sister, and him, yes. "No place in particular," he said, in response to her queries, like trying to thrill her, with verbal berries. ...was just headed into town to see if I could find a job and a place to stay and... and, and settle down. The place first, preferably, and then the job. He was heard saying this over a grunt to sit down and a sob. "A man has got to earn his keep, you know."

"Could you see yourself staying around a place like this? Maybe we could find you a job if you don't mind it here." But sis... Jarden is looking at her now, more like staring at her. Burning deep, inquiring gazes into her sister. Arms still folded across her chest of drawers, mister. She turned around and walked away while looking back now and then with nothing more to say. She's back in the house now, and the door swung shut behind her-blow-wow. "But how?" Don't ask me, Bro, go ask her, she might know! Go. No? Bernie has not yet responded to that question, and she has not said another word yet, either, except one. "Gosh!" She stops the washing and looks at him steadfastly, still looking. He looked a whole lot better already, rested, and refreshed. "Hm." She starts up again, the washing, squish, squish, squish. "They must be depending on you to find a job quickly—eh? The family must be depending on you to earn some money to send back home?" She said this while continuing to scrub away at the "suddy" wet gown.

"Ugh, no, there's no family. I'm a loner type of person, just a traveling man trying to find a place I can call home. And, and, and a job." Oh god, look! There's purpose in the scrubbing now, and another strange little sob. Lots of purposes. Look at that. Wow! She was to ask him again about finding a job around those parts. But that was to be after dinner and after dark. He accepted the dinner. That was not the only thing that he would have accepted from within her, even. Bernie was different from Shad in a myriad of ways, it would seem. Some of those were to come to light right here in this small town to gaze on, into his dreams. Unlike how things were with Shad, Bernie was not going to pass up on the chance of a night or two in a warm bed, the bag, in the hay, even. Luckily for him, the bag of hay wasn't the first thing offered up to him. It wasn't his first choice, that's so very nice, isn't it? He spent that night in a very warm bed in the house of Miss Jarden and her sister, Meighen's, and never did he ever change from that arrangement, not until the ride out of there and out of town in a tornado several decades later, as his new engagement. Well, he did change things up a bit when he had to move out of that and into this. Like, when he'd moved out of the guest room and sis, and into the master's bedroom of his, and hers, like, of their very own house. In another town not very far away from those, and into life as a married man, again. But without her knowing that much about him. Yet, he's married to her now, at this point in the game, to Mrs. Bourne, the new name. Mrs. Meighen Bourne.

Chapter 34: The Newcomers Came

Bernie sneaked into Macjacek's town but would have built up a fine family by the time he was done and gone to sit down. No one can say for sure how he left. But for sure, some tornadoes were touching down around that neck. That neck of the hood, yes, and moving on. By the time it was over, he was all gone and good, and yes, he was done with that town as we all knew he would. But he'd similarly sneaked into Jay's town, established himself quickly there as a retired soldier. He was to marry the mother of his friend's daughter. That would have been Jay's daughter, Mona, yes. Although he was twice as old as she, I guess. He was sort of doing it as a favor to one of his Cekkolandee neighbors, who was the father of Mona's one and only daughter, but her papa had to leave and go back yonder. Or was dragged back there kicking harder than a young colt being brought to order. But that man was to him more or less like a brother, so Bernie had to bother. Mr. Bourne arrived in this small town with his young wife and as someone else, quite different from themselves. Nothing about him comes close to resembling a fellow who had lived a long while before in another faraway town beyond the gated door where he'd homed in and settled down to score some more. That fellow, though, what was his name again? Bauctnumboulei or some other such funny-sounding name. Or something else for you to show to be up to speed and play the game. Or any other such thing like that, any which way, I've still got to ask. Whatever became of him? He's now, at this point in the conversation, he's at a stage where he's evolved to become Repton Turner in his own manly terms. At other times and places, though, he was Bernie Bourne, no? "No." "Yes, he was." Before that, Capo, the captain. And even further back, if one had been following him and tracking his whereabouts, one would have found him on a university campus living and studying under the name, his ever-difficult-to-pronounce name, Bauctnumboulei. If such a person was found able enough to see yet further than that, beyond the humanoid realms, perhaps, such a person might have seen him living life as a very young-looking, and a very small prince, if only in stature. But since such talents are not everyday occurrences around these parts, Sir, and grazing in these grassy hay pastures, one might never know those fact scores. In the meantime, though, the thing that he keeps closer to his heart row. This newcomer and his young family will continue to live and cultivate the farm they'd acquired there in Baker's Creek on the lot and grow corn, sweet corn, eh! Yes, you know them as The Turners, Repton Turner and his wife, and a fast-growing family. But tonight?

"Nurse!" She shouted. "It's coming." The nurse hurried over to where the young expectant mother was sitting behind her bulging stomach. Readying to deliver, and bracing herself against the hammock. Bracing her upper body backward, and yet even further back, yes, unto his laptop, Howard, that's what. The young man was with her there, useless and mortified out of his wits, I hear. Well out of his league in the current arena around these earth-land spheres. “Are you okay, dear?” He was heard asking this of her beautiful face, and fair. “Do I look okay to you? Do I look okay?” She barked back at him for saying these things. At the same time, she saw the faded-out anchor tattoo there on the wrist of Repton Turner, while giving him the eye. The nurse shot him a quick, analytical glance and made a mental note to query him further on a few things later. But not quite yet, she’s got much more urgent matters to deal with first, you bet, mi waiter. While he was taking the newborn baby out of her hands, an hour or two later, she saw her opportunity again and, of course, she did pounce upon him, like a horse. Mostly, him, aunt, not the horse, well, of course.

“Nice tats,” she said. “You wouldn’t happen to be running around with those fringe elements now, would you? Those freaks out there who are going around calling themselves what? BDV-Anchors or something like that? You’d better not be. The surest way for the child protection agency to come in and take your child, your children, even, take them all away from you.” She cast another menacing glance at him as she turned around and swiftly walked away, and out of his trailing eye view, with nothing more to say. I’m arguing this part too. Okay? Repton gulped and swallowed hard. Steaming hot he was, sweating under his T-shirt, back home to the farmyard.

Repton and his wife were a charming young couple who had recently moved into the farming community. They’d bought the old man’s farm and moved in two years earlier to cultivate the field for me. Mr. Baker, “The old man,” was the last of the Bakers’ clan to leave the Bakers Creek farming belt. His family was fast wasting away, with the Deity’s help. It was like there was a curse from the gods that had fallen on them to stay. Although theirs was one of the largest and most prominent families around those parts at first, hence the name of the place. But then comes the curse! Man, this really hurts, and tears stained the face, of course. As time passed by, it seemed as if that particular family just kept on dwindling, right before their eyes. Every generation for the last two hundred years or so would have found fewer and fewer of the Bakers left there in the region. By the time Repton and his wife were to get there to relieve them, the last of the Bakers, the current Mr. Doug Baker, was the only Baker man left there. Mr. Baker was an old and feeble man. His four children had all grown up and skipped town, all daughters, and barring none. Mr. Baker had finally come to the sad realization that he was at the end of the dynasty; he was the end of the Bakers' name, anywhere around to see. Even if he should see grandchildren of his own, like me, they will not be Bakers. That much was for sure a sound to shake, wake him up, and hurt her. So, "What's the point in carrying on," he had said. That was why he'd decided to sell out and go to bed, no?

"No. That's not how it should be said. Just go away, that's what you should say, that's how it went, okay?"

"Okay!" So, he went away while whiting off his head, to the great benefit of folks like Repton and such, as said. They bought the land, the wifely woman, and Repton. He wasted no time producing. Both in the form of crop production, the food-type of crop production, that is, as well as the other types of crop production, on a shoestring, making babies for the cribs. For example, okay, just for example, my kids. This was their second child, and the neighbors were, by then, beginning to feel somewhat more comfortable with having them around, which suited Repton just fine. Maybe he's on the way to becoming a normal, regular, everyday Joe-type of being, just like he had always wanted to be, all of the time. Before their eyes, and all his life, or more like, his many lives since arriving here on this side of the great divide. After having run headlong into the humanoid beings and their ways of doing all the many wonderful things that they do. He cannot see himself ever having to live without doing these and helping them to do it, too, ever again. He has finally arrived home, he thinks.

Chapter 35: Are They Living Amongst Us, Now?

Poetry in motion is what it is. Wow, what a message in a box of seeds, hidden away in a place like this, that, and these. Where one may find lots of rats and all those other bits of scraps, too. "Like who, do you, know...?" "No, but it's true, look up at these."

Rotting bodies waxed to a shine, gazing up at ancient corpses wrapped up in twine, and went dazed from looking at them for days. Wasting away, the longer they stay. Tears calling, emotionally falling to pieces in torment and decay. Unsocially, worms and mots picked rapidly at the cups, although upright on two, those two were to have stood up, like you.

Strange sightings have been showing up in and around humanoid space, a place called Earth, and home, of late. Seen folks living where servers and pretenders in eateries and bar-tenders are doctoring food in the weirdest of ways, presenting "Noods." Now don't ask, "What's that?" Because that's rude, and you're not that hot, nobody can accuse you of being that type of food, from the pots.

They're bringing it in, dressed up and with frills, before half-starved gills in restaurants and diners down there on the corners, food that kills. Meanwhile, said folks are quickly losing their taste for home-cooked meals, arguing their dissatisfaction over discounts and your inattention to details. For not applying the deals as were offered on resale. While raising hell, upsetting those who were doctoring fries and bringing them before them on platters to enjoy.

While banging angry arms on counters and ringing the bells. "Oh boy!" "Yay," they say, "What a joy. Now it's good, okay, I'll be coming again, for more of this; the right type of food", now, hiss and send. Good.

Look at them, there they are; zombie-like bodies between the cars. They and their daddies are walking our streets. "Or not quite walking, are they, on the beats?" "No." But getting by on irregular contraptions and gadgets to reach...

When crooks, pirates, and snake oil salesmen rush in to set up shady schemes to seduce and to snatch, friend. Separating people from their money and hard-earned cash to spend. With trickery, too, and adding some feel-good dash at them.

When churches are made to become killing fields, the powers that be don't see a gun issue with which to deal. Rather, a mental health issue, and still, they go on pretending and selling you that pill. But could it be that they are amongst the mentally ill? Are they living among us, still?

Some weird-looking beings have been showing up here in recent times, and altered stately gear. Which seem to be floating about on two and in upright mobile forms carried by air. But slightly, or slightly more than slightly off-balance, they are. Cross-walking still, against the car. Now, tell me, are they? Really, are they like, like, living?

Which leaves one to wonder at times, are these even humans at all? Are they of the earthling kind to crawl? How secure is that call? Hmm, hmm, and humming yet some more, Paul, while walking along through the mall. Whereas on this side of the great divide, one may be accustomed to seeing earthlings in their goings, going about walking, upright on two things, side by side to do, new swings.

Legs, they're called, I think, or some other such dancing, walking thing. Feet, maybe, or something else like that thing taken with tea. "And buttered biscuit fat, Leigh?" Yes, and that, as I hear tell-tales of it, was to become the established normal habit.

However, in recent times, on the river. There have been reports coming out of their behinds to deliver, which tends to leave some of them and their ancestors' kind, a bit more than slightly disturbed over there near the spotted blinds. Reports of some rather strange sightings, out there on the hood, unsightly graffiti writings. Isn't there a cause for these harsh writings? "Yes, because it's the right thing."

Sightseeing some beings appearing among them whose "walking" motion runs alarmingly counter-course, and contrary to those established norms, of course, it's not good. Cause for alarms, now they're unglued.

Whereas that was the norm over there for beings of those same humanoid kinds to care, and go about walking upright on two feet. Putting one of those things in front of the other, and the other one behind you. "Neath." Those things on which they would move about further, and go wandering, from place to place, and yet further, in your face.

Lift them up and put them down, one in front of the other, heels and toes round. While lunging themselves forward to get from point A to point B, and all the while with a synchronized movement for us to see, of the other upper limbs towards me, hands, they call them, I've heard. Or arming some other thing like that nerd.

Those upper limbs, afore times, back and forward, too, would likely have been moving in line, like, in sync with the lower thing of thine. The one on this side of the being would have been moving opposite to the one on that side of the same. Simultaneously, were those movements in the divided game.

As the upper and lower limbs would have been moving likewise, yeah, yes, Stephen. Opposite one to the other one-eyed void in a very synchronized and smooth manner, that's the reason, Mama. Which would have rendered it effortless and smooth, more like poetry in motion. "Nude?" "No, don't be rude." Of late, however, reports have been coming out and over, and it's not all good, surely, not clever.

Off-balance they are, and out of whack. Makes you want to tear your eyes out and say, wtf? Our ancestors had taken a peek down from the windows of time and home. They were to have marveled at what came a-crawling up his "behind" tailbone. Yes, his behind, the offspring kind, not the ancestors' to leave us denying.

The form of his offspring leaves him to wonder in grandeur; from whence did this kind come down yonder? From me, they sure have not descended, no wonder. Because they bear no resemblance to me nor to what I once used to be, I can't be a pretender. "I see," so said he, but these in no way looked or acted like me.

The way they go about doing things ought not to be. The upper stumps of them have grown elongated and out of whack. The sitting points on the hind side seem overweight and showed a crack. Speak with a lisp as if he'd lost his tongue. Walks with spread legs as if a pole is wedged up where he "Siddung." Sorry, I meant to say, go over there and sit down.

Another of the ancestors would have looked in there and was surprised to see. Nothing is working as it once used to be. Lying and cheating in these times have become the norm. The one who does the right thing is ridiculed and scorned. One man treats the other man like a brute, while he goes about amending laws and debating the truth.

In olden times, you'd elect and send to the House your representatives to represent you, your interests, and the way you live. Nowadays, it's to those lawmakers you have, those great powers given, to give. And in crying, you cursed, flowing rivers of tears. Because the laws those lawmakers make are theirs, bringing you to the mountains, yes, mountains of fear.

Brighten your "Now" countenance, but leave you worse for wear. He only comes around your corner when it's an election year, while he and his cronies mount up and climb high on the golden stairs. Here, yes, go have a beer, I guess. Because, in lying, it is a thing no such leader lacks, looks you square in the "balls" and sells you a pack.

This is where the weasel bumps are upon the creepers' weaker spinal track. Right, there is the center spot of attention for that eel to sack it. In that, there seems to be no lack of the key to the lock and to unlock the locket. Got it yet? "Yes." Alright then. Amen.

There they go again, that man now begets children who place their safety in other people's hands, along with everything else that they would have planned. Well, all except those things he wants from you to nyam. Go on, eat it, don't you let me repeat it. Now go on, back to that one, and this. You do it, it's your job to make everything work right for me and fit. So said that man as if he and his children's pickney dem are living, but are they, like, are they living among us? Again?

They walked around with their eyes fixed on gadgets in their palm. Wouldn't waste a gaze at one on the right hand, unless it's to do him in, with harm. Or even the one on the left of them, because he's having an important conversation with a friend whom he has never met from Adam, though he lives just across the world in a foreign nation.

Whatever you do, buddy, don't interrupt this conversation I'm having with my friends from across town. Even though here in this city, of that kind, I've got none. Don't you dare stop me, don't block my way. I'm walking a straight line here, can't you see and obey? Don't make me have to turn to this side or go the other way.

If a wall should fall before me, tall. I'll hop over it or even crawl. If you should ever stick up before me a long pole, I'll cut you through with my fierce indignation, or push you down the hole. Then record it all onto my instant camera and send it off to every living soul. So they will see you lying there dying in a pool of blood at the base of a stake, or stranded at the root of a pole. No one bothered to lend a hand; they couldn't be bothered with the rigmarole.

I can do whatever I want to, add as much shock value to it as I feel like to. Do you in even, but whatever you do, don't be shocked by that and react, or it will be all your fault, and you will be responsible for whatever you do. Or not do, on the asphalt, and you only, pal. I have nothing to do with it, nor with that gal. "No, it wasn't me, Shaggy." Even though you might have been shocked out of your wits by what I said when I did it. It's still all your fault, admit it, and yours only. Are they living among us?

A generation that curses its elders. The aged among them are ridiculed and scorned because they know nothing and should be long gone. "Needs fresh ideas," because you're old and redundant. Take the running of their affairs and place it in the hands of infants.

Dust your face with a powdered-looking glass, then tell them they're nice and you know, they'll pass. Break the pop champagne, man must floss. Waste the Rodman because correction is a thing of the past. Because we are in the know, born that way, it's how we flow. Now hand over the doe and go.

Wear chapped jeans if I please, below 40 degrees, and go pink at the knees. Because I'm free, don't you dare talk down to me. One might be tempted to ask you and say: It's not everybody that you are having issues with that way, just him who is unmitigated enough to try and lift you from there, out of the dust, and from the pit of muck and toilet wear. With those words, of course, I swear. But as for you? To try and lift you, perhaps, you're surely going to have some issues with that. Are they even living?

"Don't talk down to us," another man said. Then send you off to go to bed, and to sleep. Weep. So you're acknowledging that the place where you are is down, right? And that the place where that man is talking to you from is at a higher place than where you are rebuffing him? Bright.

So, am I allowed to ask that rhetorical question of the past, again? What is that thing that makes you want to become so comfortable at that low place? Why are you now so ready to go dragging the man down to the low place where you are, in the waste? For no other reason than for him to have the unmitigated gall to try and lift you from there, perhaps? Beware. Friend, beware.

Could it be that there are interested parties with a vested interest in having you in a lowly place and tumbling down yet further with the expensive car keys? One who's very skilled at the art of getting you and yours to think just like he wants you to think, on these? And you're busily doing his bidding even now? Wow!

There he is, telling you that you're really that, and this. Could that be the same "someone" person right there, and fat like puss, square? Hissed. Could he be just a bit interested in dumbing you down and succeeding at it, fast? Telling you about self-esteem and the other bits, and sending you nearer my god to the corner beam to hang your head and sit?

"Let no one talk down to you," he said. Which seemed to some folks I know to mean, listen to me and to what I tell you, mi bred. Don't let anybody else tell you anything, like when to go to bed or what to do. Wake you up, too, with a gaslighting finger on the queue. Slanting truths across sharp knives to cut them through, by surprise. Not even those who love and care for them, and like, like, the most?

I'm the only one you need to hear because I'm the only one who cares. Care for, and about you, over here, man. True? "True." Yeah! Right, and why? Because I said so, guy, gimme a light, man. Phew. And, and... puff, I can prove it, too. Look at how I make you feel: Powerful, valued, worthwhile, and shit, look at it this way, puff, and sniff. Okay, cough, cough, now spit, then continue with it.

They're nothing to you, can help you none. They're old and know nothing; they're already done, you and I are up and coming, fresh, clean, nice, and young. We now know everything and have the world in the palm of our hands to swing. We don't need them, no, not even in the least, my friend. Go. That is how they flow.

"You do it, go on now, or go away." Go out and fix it for me, make me feel safe and shit, see? "Yes," so that I may walk around doing nothing to quit, with my mind out of it, as my eyes are always focused on my gadget. Since you already know that that is how it goes, it's you who has to go out and make sure that I'm secure, like...

Like whenever I go about, like, to go shopping for things to buy in every store of yours, and much, much, and even much more, of course. It's you who must make sure to do all those things that you've got to do for me. Don't you see? You had better be very sure to open up every door of the opportunity store, and let me in way before, you know, like.

Before I freeze out here in this cold weather that I did not dress properly for... why should I bother when I can pass off this responsibility to another? Or dump it over your shoulder. "Cause?" Because you're older and don't have much further to go, other than to show that you know, that I'm in style, and you're done spoiled. You don't want me to go and file...

"Like what?"

"File a suit against you, Yute." So said the young youth to me, and you. For in failing, you failed to do what you already knew you ought to for me. You'll soon see what shall become of thee. I don't have to do anything, I've got you to do it all for me, if anything, even to think, and the kitchen sink. You do it, I quit. Now puff, phew, and spit. Look at him, blowing out what's left of you and his cigarette. Are they living among us?

As is now the custom, this overly tattooed generation can barely answer one out of two questions. Sometimes he's right, but sometimes he gets it wrong, both of them, even. But he's answering yet, he's a confident one, you bet. Self-operated devices and machinery are theirs, because such are preferred and trusted over and above you and me in the car. Us... of their very own kind, I swear, who had designed and built it, fuss. "Us?" Yes, it was we and our kind who had built it in the first place, though, wasn't it so? "Yes." But there they go, are they living among us?

No compassion, no empathy. No feeling of love for the man, not anybody. Or concerns towards each other. No love for the man who is his brother. "No, that's not his brother, but yours." "I know, I know, so, you are?" They gleefully eat up glistening white snow, the one on the lot with the heavenly glow they'd picked up from the side of the road not long ago.

Not remembering that that was where they had seen the pile of dirty black snow, not many days ago. And that's how this beautiful white pile is going to look in just a little while. But you're in style, so go on and smile a while, you're on Candid Camera, my child. Whatever you do. Don't ever think, flush that wasted stink down the sink, and blink, rapidly now.

Are they living among us? It makes me wonder sometimes; there must be somebody somewhere working on us. Or over us, under us, even. Working undercover after all, covering up a stink, under all of that ink, yeah! All of that: Tattoo ink. Now, go on. Wink.

Chapter 36: Spinners in the Alps Soup

Beahon and Angel would have met up halfway down the road or up the road, depending on whose point of view you are looking at it from and seeing things through. Angie's moving on up to the top. Well, not quite that far up to the top, just as far up to where Beahon had stopped to meet her on the way down the back. Beahon doesn't seem to like it that much up there as at home, and has opted to take a leg or two with him on the way back down. You do know that he could have lost both, though, don't you? Just like how some folks would have lost their hearts in some Frisco, to you. I mean, in some frisky part of town, or two. Or he could have fared even worse. He could have been forced to divorce his headship of the house, like some of the other house-mouses, perhaps. Well, nice, Sis, of course, and get to step down below his neck while watching them as they mess around, "What the heck." Messing with the wreck on his head near the bed up there, as said. Nothing to spare, mi bred, I swear. But he really seems to have found some favor with the Kingsley bunch. Sorry, I meant to say, with King Liam, Ooh. Okay? Yes. He really loved that man. Must have been something that they had fixed him up with, and placed it right there in his lunch kit to nyam. He dug in and ate up all of it. So when he was given the choice, he would have opted to take the boys and then the plunge. Going on down into a more homely setting, down home, to eat his lunch. Said he felt a lot more comfortable among lowly people. Sorry, Mr. King, I meant no evil. I meant to say, Your Royal Highness, sorry. I didn't mean to imply that they are "lowly" at all; they're not. They're Cekko people after all, on the lot. So now Angie and Beahon are there, settling in nicely on a chair in the upper echelon of Cekko's societal air. You all know that Beahon was just a boy then, just a little more than a baby hen. No, not a chick, get with it. Go, run guh dund-a bredda Joe guh get the "likkle" money fei flow and come back quickly, quick. So, maybe, maybe when they'd brainwashed him. Sorry, I meant to say, trained him, like. If they had trained him. They would have squeezed him into the A-chamber and out again. Do you remember? "No?" Well, listen up, what the hell! Go. Maybe like you, he'd never managed to learn a thing, nor two. Not much about the real Cekko thing, or the how-to. Like how to do things, how to behave and act in the presence of kings, "I will never be comfortable with those types of things." So said he to the king's men and... yes, them. So, back down low, he'd much rather go than waste yet more years there trying to know. Trying to learn these kinds of things and to show them that he doesn't need to know, not that much so... "I'm going to go down low before I get older," so said the little rock band from Beahon to the boulder. Got my coat now over my shoulder. Angie baby, Angie baby, here I come. You're a pretty little woman, babe, and I want to give you some. You know, like, something nice and very well done. You know that the Cekko people never die, though, right? Well, at least some of them on some nights, so, tell... what the hell's up with this bright light? Are you coming in to get me tonight? Go away! Anyway, they need to bargain this out really tightly. Bargaining with heads screwed on the right, Leigh. Though some lips could have been chopped off, more or less like liver, and given over to whoever. They'd still have to bargain, though, and with clever, yes, like, cleverness, like so. To decide which half would get custody of the eye and sight? "Seen." No, that's Jamaican "yardman sin ting, or something aggen," ...and keep it hidden. See what I mean? The lower parts got the better half after all. So now she's the bigger boss and he, yes, him? He can look back over it all, and see, and grin. See what's happening to you and me? And-and... Stop! Hey! Did you hear that? Listen up fast, listen. "Wooooo." There it is again, the roaring, wailing sound blowing in the wind. It's becoming a regular thing of late, and it's usually followed up closely by a tornado or a hurricane in its wake. Guess Smokey is at it again, sitting up late and wiping his slate clean. Or at least, he's trying to be mean. Smokey has been hanging there all these many centuries, decades, and years, too. Spinning away on things and spinning his wares and tears, on you. In some ways, he's spinning around on that long string for days. That string that the king would have graciously given to him, one day, while he was on the way out to look for and find his spouse and queen.

Among all other such royal things, I would have heard it tell-say. If only he had remembered to grab his kit when he had to run for it, before Cekkonians would have awakened to find him quit and gone. No, don't yawn. Step it up, man, and gwaan, galang. Sorry, I meant to say, carry on. Otherwise, go away. Can't stop now, we're almost home to pasture the cow, and to stay, but not in lockdown as it is now known, in our day.

Meanwhile, Bauctnumboulei is out there having a blast, going about performing many tasks, not caring one iota about such things. Surely, not for how long it may last (or may not last). They've got the watch he knows. His time, though, will last, that's for sure. He still trots the globe doing his tasks, such as these, since you'd asked. Like gardening, planting seeds, and weeding. Everywhere and fast came the cross-breeding. A daughter here, sons over there, and fitting them well into the strategic square. Some are hiding in sperm... E. banks, and specializing in medical care. Caring for the facilities, and for his several abilities, such as these. What is it now? What do you see? Did you hear that coming from him?

"Who?"

"Him, that one from over there in Cekkoland, my king, or was it two?" Listen, listen to him, coming through on the line-in. ...and wait, he will wait there, long. Yes, he will. He most certainly will. "...Yes, you must wait, even if it's 'till thy kingdom come,' and it will, SON. It shall be done."

Meanwhile. "Sit down, nuh servant," said King Liam to his newfound longtime friend. The Shadow Man, again. The storm had passed. The dust had cleared, and there was a new normal being established in Cekkoland in general and in the kingdom over there, and fast. As of this point, it seemed as if there would be no more firstborn sons of the kings to ascend the throne before the taking off of the fathers for the ascent up to the most exalted realms. Bauctnumboulei is gone, on to another sphere. He's not expected to be back to reign in Cekkoland any time soon, if ever, over there. There are some other princes now added, by way of the search and recovery program that the king had requested and sanctioned into being. Every one of those things over on the scene is now packed tightly in and padded. But none of those would have the desired prerequisites to become kings, not according to the established standards as known over there in the Cekkoland realms. None of these were or could in any way be passed off as being firstborn children. So, new codes and uploads, among other roads, I suppose, now happening under their robes, and their sniffing noses, too, like the smell of roses. True.

The Shadow Man is closer to the king than any had ever been before. He's living there with him in the palace, behind closed doors. No more malice, as before. The talking conversations seemed everlasting. They never stop talking and smoking the chalice. Who's asking? "Me."

"Sit down, servant."

"No, you know I can't sit down." Man, I'm so overjoyed. "Suh wah fih mek yu fih kyaan siddung? Sorry, that yardie man sin ting aggen. But the king? Listen to him."

"What is to prevent you from being able to sit down, man? "Sit down, that's a command. Do you still want to go on?"

"No?"

"I thought so. What is this, though? What's this nonsense?"

"Just an earthling thing, and then some. Like, a song they like to sing over there, to someone. You know the earthlings, they like to sing a lot and offer praises to their gods, and the stars, among other things, as they are. No, no, Nannette, not those stars, but the performance types of stars. Singers and actors, or maids at the bar. But preachers and teachers? As for them, they are—"No, don't bother," so said he, to his brother. "Unruly bunch? Seems like it to me. Are you ready for lunch?"

"No, maybe after tea."

"...you'd better not be, though, you'd better not be like them if you're planning on hanging around with him. You know, like, with me, your king."

"But, but."

"No, stop that, that's enough, no more butting buts."

"Can't I go back, though? I mean, I really want to go."

"No, you can't go, not anymore."

"You do know that I've got interests there, though, real interests? Like those, like spouses, and children whom I must go back and bless, and who need arouse... trousers and a dress. You do know that, don't you?"

"Yes, I know, and I still say, you can't go, that's an order." But the Shadow man was already getting up and preparing to leave and go across the border, "you know—" "Sit down, servant, I said, sit down." Too out of order.

"I knew it, I knew it. You're jealous (Spit). Bet you're sitting there and sorry-moaning over the fact that it was me who had gone out there and met all those wonderful folks and would have gotten to see, yeah! To see and do all of those wonderful things. Bet you're there wishing and hoping that it was you, and not me."

"No, I'm not, and if I wanted to, I could have, yes, I could have gone out. Even now, it's not too late for me to go. If I want to, I can, and stop fooling yourself with that one; it wasn't you who had gone out there and done all those things. Not on your own account, as to you, so it might have seemed. You were sent, remember? And guess who it was that had sent you? Yes, you've guessed it right, it was me."

"But you're sorry now, say it isn't so, say it isn't so."

"Sit down, servant, and stop pushing it; keep pushing the envelope as you do, and you'll find out soon. It will come pushing back hard at you, Shad. I'm warning you."

"Alright, alright, I heard you, man. I heard you the first time, too. But come on. Bet you wish sometimes, though, that you had taken the trip to go. That you had gone out there yourself instead of sending me, no?"

"No. Bet you're wrong on that, too. It's not half bad here, you should know that. But I guess too much time has passed since you have not been here. That, too, however, can be fixed, and could be up and running well before we are to be over here and..." Done.

WritingElk.

Now, here's an excerpt from my next book in the series. Just for you, and me.

Team players

Peace! Just asking this. What peace were they talking about, sis? There was no peace for weeks in the house out east. Even in the very best of times and stout feet look fine. There was no peace for many to find and go fine-tune the patch of thyme, each week. A select few have some semblance of it in truth, yes, yes, my youth. And all else that they were to get, they have it. Such and such at their fingertips. Hey there! Get the clipper and cut this. Yes, that's it. Now, continuing on with the speech. Sheamus was lucky to have been counted amongst them, plus nine is more when ten comes around to hang with them. You know, the plus-sized guys in the world's admiring eyes. The more those select few got, the more they wanted to spend on craps. You know them! Amen. Until not much was left anywhere for the rest of the pair of go-getters there, to go out and get theirs. Nor for the scared stiff out of their neat wheats types of bringers to come bringing in to feather their neat nested hens over the eggs here. Those sitting on the egg where? Yes, there. Beware. Because. As opposed to how such things were to go with the have-nots. That was when they started looking elsewhere for ways to balance out the lopsided scaled-up chair, again, on props. And yet more in their favor was to be the blame, such a shame. Or if there remain other warm, red watery veins stained yet unclaimed by the deadly pain. They must go find that other place to become their savior's game-changing playing fame. Like, a new planet again. That was when all the roads led to a survival town with no name. Nestled somewhere out there amongst the hornets' rain, as it was known to them then. Where the fittest of the fittest, and the quickest of the quick, go to get it. Like, whatever there may be for them to get off that, and this. When trouble comes hanging around that wretched neck of his, and starts to settle in on their own doorstep, kids, that too. To view the baby lying there in the crib by you. Not only theirs, but firstly so. True? True. All of the others were to follow through, and then came you. No?

So, in fighting, they had to fight. For the right to the living of their life. Their lives, only. Up until the few came down to two, as seen through Sheamus' eyes, that he was looking through. That wasn't how they'd planned it, though, give them the benefit of that pop E-show. They didn't plan to wipe out the whole worldly fam in truth, like scouts would sometimes do it to the youth. But there was a fluke thrown into the pan coot, and out came that brute to shoot; bang bang. Then came the sabotage, and now... from amongst the "some," others were to come. Then, from amongst those "ones" too, come these two. Among the remaining pained few, but this much, they never knew. Well, there may yet be others out there somewhere. That is the hope for this Sheamus and friend pair. See them there? Look, they're sitting right there on starvation square. That's the hook. But that's where they're intent on going, footing it bare. No, not to starvation square again. They're already there in heaven... yeah! Well, say amen. "Amen," but. There they are, going, the dog and he... Slowing. To go find what's left of them. Yes, those other far-away friends with no name as known to them. He just says: "Hey, how are you, my friend?" whenever he runs into them, but. He wanted to even up the score with Essence, his friend, on tour. That's why the walking shoes are now hanging behind his back door. Cute! Cute. Swinging from his crooked stick on his poor shoulder, his back heavily laden, to a sick, on the bent crooked end of it. Yes, of his walking stick. Look. Out into a hopeful village. Look, they're headed now.

Searching for... Hoof, hoof, blow-wow. But, but. Listen up now, yardie sin thing aggen.

But what now? How did good, going sorts of living things ever get this good long-distance line away from the properly good living kind anyway? Chickens were coming home to roost, I'd say. The comfort zone had come falling and tumbled down one day. It had finally fallen off their miserable, sorry, I meant to say, miserly crown foot on the clay near the doorway.

Team players were the games of the day, oh, you've all been played now, I'd say -my friends, like so. Losing out on the winning dice throw. Such a shame, though. The good times had run their course. For the good livers, of course. Things were getting from bad to worse as they were seeing things by way of the empty purse. The stuffy chest panting rancid air they no longer wanted was even worse for wares. They were to be heard increasingly complaining and cursing the clerks at the Days Inn, where. Those who were shirking work there at the clubhouse evenings, and even worse than that thing, one two three times out and in? Yes. I'm leaving, on a jet... But first, let's finish the reading. Like, yes. They were complaining at the posh gathering places near Stevens, nurse, was what they named him. The jetsetters were getting upset and staying sweatier than wet. Somewhere under the collar, there near the upper neck tier. Where? There, somewhere under the cloth of some sort of chest gear. Meanwhile, every day Joey types of fellowshipping people slight, slipped one-handed onto the slowly weeping knives of the knights, and were just on the verge of a breakthrough from under the cellar sellers' plight. As seen through dry yeye pickney dem. With those bratty children picking a fight with me, and you too, my friend. As I'm here trying to find the right way to say and do the things to do? It's like. They were getting closer to being the sellers of cellphones to call her down home, perhaps, and to give one of these things to her to give to you, on the swaps. Which never came through as the said seller fellow would have preferred it to do. As soon as he reaches out his anxious fingers to grab a supporting role of the dice upon his dinner, bibblinngg!

came the ringing sin ting, no, not the telephone sort. But, something like that wart. It was the fork dropping out of his finger gripping… Rinnnngg! Oh cloth. There it goes again. I wonder why it's so bent on falling when… You know, not when but from. From the thing holding him in. The darned thing just slips out of his grasping grips just like that shilling there, and this. Some new crisis or another dice-like just happened to pop up out of the blue lagoon abyss, bladder, again. Just like this one-sided pain. Even. Which was to slap the harshest of setback king spells upon you and him to go sell to the rest of them. Perhaps. Or to the next Bydened bidding newcomer coming in, in kind, to unpack. Instead of the ringing thing you and he'd wanted him to bring, or to send it in. Those who, as it turned out, could scarcely find a pocketing dime to talk about. Or, even to spend on thyme shout "yes!" hallelujah! Well, I guess. I'll give that much to y'all. The people wanted answers, so that was what they got from her. Whether or not it was a workable one, sir. It was, in fact, a hamster. Look at it, there, isn't it cute? I swear! Yes, yes, it is — my yute man pickney, dear. But to be fair. To many it seemed feasible, like what they had promised to give him and you, in spite, so. The plan was set in motion to go. It was designed so that all the world's population, growth, or none. Could come together and go out, or come. To go work towards a common feathery goal-lee golden golden-feathered plan, yes, mi beloved bredda man. That one was preferred, oh, over any other one, so. Reasonable enough. No? Well, go. The leaders and elders of each nation-notion stood tough-tough. Ruff enough. Standing up on the easiest sellers selling the plan from the rough, land "ding" on your hand. They formed alliances with everyone that they could get their handles on. Like, them and you to hitch a ride on us and get on through, in comfort. The political class wasn't going through the cast, nor were they ever going to be found left out of the acting axe man with his one act to perform. Not even these two men with two axes to send off their arms to you. So they too went and signed a packed queue like this. Ewew! Regularly, they were to meet up to plan the reconstruction. For a while, things went well enough, yes, my Child. Now. Nuh mek mi haffi cuss. Enough of that style. Stop before you're overly spoiled. Okay. What can I say? But there was another plan hidden somewhere in the shut-pan anyway. Known by one and allowed via some sass to the rest of his clan and such. But now, the clan is down to one, because of the mashallah that was brought on.

The rest of the goners from that corner are all gone now, in the minds of those few left in command, somehow, so they thought. But in fact, there was a crack in the sack box. Because. There are many still locked up under the sander. Somewhere in a far corner of the Kingsland ore. I think they're those who were calmer than this one door ring one here, or the two of them to make up the walking pair. Somebody knew the new sounding gear, from a long time down home. Even. Knew that these few could be made liable to become reliable, and so they were made able to understand the fable, like. How to take command from the other men, yes, man. That was the real, reasoned-out plan to let them live on among a few of the other men and this one. Those were never to be among the goners in the van farmer. This they had decided upon. In the concluding minds of a select few of the stormer kind. Yes, the bull bucket kicking ram farming kind had also signed in. But for the most part, that was no threat to start, that's why I'm in. Hence the plan to save for them the bounce back day when...

Those people were drugged and laid away, starting with little children—okay? Children who were stolen away from the field of play. Whilst their parents worried and pined away. "Bring back our children home," they say. But, how did they come to fall upon such bad luck? With the made-up thing from the doctor's cup? Perhaps, take a sup, drink, drink. Drink it up.

Just an excerpt from book #2, it's coming soon. Thank you.

E Lloyd Kelly is an Author, Poet, and podcaster.

Other works by E Lloyd Kelly, is on E K's Amazon bookshelf:

o Poetic Just Ice, Cold

o The Shi t Depot

o The sword, the word, and the writings (free giveaway on site) o Training Manley. And

o Spaces: My space, your space, and the public space. Among others.

These are also available on the Author's page at Amazon.com/author/elloydkelly, or https://www.amazon.com/E.-LloydKelly/e/B01G7NYWL6

E K would like to hear from his readers. Email him at contact, elkthepoet@gmail.com.

"Note from the author" Just a note of thank you for choosing to read my book and for sticking with it even to the very end. You must have liked it a lot. At this point, I want to ask you, my reader, my friends, to take a minute or two to post a review of the book on the sales pages at Amazon and any other such sales pages. This small gesture is so very much appreciated. And don't keep it to yourself, be sure to share the love. Tell someone. Thank you.

More notes: some small lines and quotes in this book may be recognized as familiar lines from some well-known (or not-too-well-known) songs. We lay no claim to the ownership of these materials, and only use them on a presumption of "fair use" basis, and out of pure love and admiration for the pieces and in some cases, the authors and other individuals in others. Should the rights owners have issues with our usage of any of these pieces, just let us know and we will take the necessary efforts to rectify the situation, or remove the offending pieces, as may be possible in some cases nowadays too. Thank you very much.

Special thanks also go out to those people who have helped in various ways in bringing about this book. Thanks to my immediate as well as the extended families: To Leonie and Charles who had to put up with me not being quite there at times, even when I might have been there in the body. In the end, your support was unwavering and unmistakable. Thank you. To my church family who supported me by allowing me the time, space, and also physically, by spending your hard-earned cash to purchase the books or by telling others about them. Thank you.

So, why do I write? The answer is this:

I'm a guy of many words, but whose tongue is slow and heavy. My words tend to come out awkward and clumsy. So, I write, because I always have something to say, I think. Which always tends to get me into trouble anyway. Yes, that's why I write. The extra bonus though, which comes by writing, is that a pencil usually comes with an eraser.

E Lloyd Kelly is an Author, poet, podcaster, and blogger. Born in Jamaica, West Indies, to Raglan and Alma Kelly. Now resides in Montreal, Quebec.

Keep the mind sharp, read something, anything, but we sure would love it if you do read our books. Take a look. At, amazon.com/author/elloydkelly

#readabooktoday #realinkytrail.

www.ingramcontent.com/pod-product-compliance
Lightning Source LLC
Chambersburg PA
CBHW072051110526
44590CB00018B/3130